Redefining Teacher Education

Rethinking Childhood

Joe L. Kincheloe and Janice A. Jipson
General Editors

Vol. 20

PETER LANG
New York • Washington, D.C./Baltimore • Bern
Frankfurt am Main • Berlin • Brussels • Vienna • Oxford

Diane D. Orlofsky

Redefining Teacher Education

The Theories of Jerome Bruner and the Practice of Training Teachers

PETER LANG
New York • Washington, D.C./Baltimore • Bern
Frankfurt am Main • Berlin • Brussels • Vienna • Oxford

LIBRARY OF CONGRESS CATALOGING-IN-PUBLICATION DATA

Orlofsky, Diane D.
Redefining teacher education: the theories of Jerome Bruner
and the practice of training teachers / Diane D. Orlofsky.
p. cm. — (Rethinking childhood; vol. 20)
Includes bibliographical references (p.   ) and index.
1. Teachers–Training of–United States. 2. Bruner, Jerome S. (Jerome
Seymour)–Views on learning. 3. Teachers colleges–United
States–Curricula. I. Title. II. Series.
LB1715 .O74   370'.71'173–dc21   00-064762
ISBN 0-8204-5187-8
ISSN 1086-7155

DIE DEUTSCHE BIBLIOTHEK-CIP-EINHEITSAUFNAHME

Orlofsky, Diane D.:
Redefining teacher education: the theories of Jerome Bruner
and the practice of training teachers / Diane D. Orlofsky.
–New York; Washington, D.C./Baltimore; Bern;
Frankfurt am Main; Berlin; Brussels; Vienna; Oxford: Lang.
(Rethinking childhood; Vol. 20)
ISBN 0-8204-5187-8

Cover design by Joni Holst

The paper in this book meets the guidelines for permanence and durability
of the Committee on Production Guidelines for Book Longevity
of the Council of Library Resources.

Printed in the United States of America

Table of Contents

Figures

Acknowledgments

I owe debts of gratitude to many people, not the least of whom is the late Martha Harris Wurtz. When she handed me a copy of Bruner's *The Process of Education*, she could not have anticipated the intellectual journey that would follow. She, and many other former teachers, cared enough to invest in my academic/professional growth. Sincere appreciation is extended to them all—with special recognition to Dr. David Matson and Dr. Amy Brown.

Special thanks to Reba Allen for her help with the figure designs used in this text and to Donald R. Norsworthy for the author photo. Thanks to my student, Rob Lyda, for his editorial assistance. Sincere appreciation to Heidi Burns, Jeff Galas, and Lisa Dillon of Peter Lang Publishing for their guidance and input.

This project was launched with the help of the American Association of University Women American Fellows Program. Many thanks to this fine organization and to Troy State University for its cooperation and support. Appreciation is also extended to the Harvard University Archives.

Thanks to my former students, Frieda Davis Bullard, Ward Thigpen, and Beverly McCall for the use of their conceptual maps.

To my parents, my first teachers. Thank you for a lifetime of encouragement.

To my husband, Mike, my partner, cheerleader, and first reader. You have made me a better writer and a better person. Many thanks with love and respect.

To my children, Anna and Elizabeth. It is my greatest privilege to be your mother. I learn from you both daily and you have made me a more compassionate teacher.

I would also like to gratefully acknowledge these copyright holders and thank them for granting permission to use passages from the following works:

Jerome S. Bruner, On learning mathematics. *The Mathematics Teacher, 53(8)*. Reston, VA: National Council of Teachers of Mathematics, 1960. Reprinted by permission of the publisher. All rights reserved.

Jerome S. Bruner, Structures in learning. *NEA Journal, 52(3)*. Washington, DC: National Education Association, 1963. Reprinted by permission of the publisher. All rights reserved.

Jerome S. Bruner, Theorems for a theory of instruction. In J. S. Bruner (Ed.), *Learning about learning: A conference report*, 1966, pp. 196–210. ERIC Document Reproduction Service No. ED 015 492. Reprinted by permission of the author. All rights reserved.

Jerome S. Bruner, Notes on divisive dichotomies. In T. Holland and C. Lee (Eds.), *The alternative of radicalism: Radical and conservative possibilities for teaching the teachers of America's young children*, pp. 48–61. From the Conference of the Tri-University Project, 1969. ERIC Document Reproduction Service No. ED 046 941. Reprinted by permission of the author. All rights reserved.

Jerome S. Bruner, The relevance of skill or the skill of relevance. In M. E. Meyer and F. H. Hite (Eds.), *The First Western Symposium on Learning: The application of learning principles to classroom instruction*, pp. 4–13. Bellingham, WA: Western Washington University, 1971. Reprinted by permission of the publisher. All rights reserved.

Jerome S. Bruner, *The relevance of education*. Copyright ©1971 by Jerome S. Bruner. Used by permission of W. W. Norton & Company, Inc. All rights reserved.

Jerome S. Bruner, Jerome S. Bruner. In Gardner Lindzey (Ed.), *History of Psychology in Autobiography, Volume 7*, 1980, pp. 75–151. San Francisco: W. H. Freeman. Copyright ©1990 by Gardner Lindzey. Reprinted by permission of the editor. All rights reserved.

Jerome S. Bruner, Models of the learner. *Educational Researcher, 14(6)*. Washington, DC: American Educational Research Association, 1985. Copyright ©1985 by the American Educational Research Association. Reprinted by permission of the publisher. All rights reserved.

Jerome S. Bruner, Science education and teachers: A Karplus lecture. *Journal of Science Education and Technology, 1(1)*. New York: Plenum Publishing Corporation, 1992. Reprinted by permission of the publisher. All rights reserved.

Jerome S. Bruner, What we have learned about early learning. *European Early Childhood Education Research Journal, 4*(1). United Kingdom: Centre for Research in Early Childhood, University College Worcester, 1996. Reprinted by permission of the publisher. All rights reserved.

Jerome S. Bruner, Private Papers, Harvard University Archives (4242.xx) Reprinted by permission of the author. All rights reserved.

Jerome S. Bruner & B. Clinchy. In J. S. Bruner (Ed.), *Learning about learning: A conference report*, 1966, pp. 71–83. ERIC Document Reproduction Service No. ED 015 492. Reprinted by permission of the author. All rights reserved.

Linda Darling-Hammond, Educating teachers: The academy's greatest failure or its most important future. *Academe, 85*(1). Washington, DC: American Association of University Professors, 1999. Reprinted by permission of the publisher. All rights reserved.

Diane DeNicola, In memoriam. *Proteus: A Journal of Ideas, 8*(1). Shippensburg, PA: Shippensburg University, 1991. Copyright © 1991 by Shippensburg University. Reprinted by permission.

Diane DeNicola Orlofsky, Cavemen used music like phones. *The National Forum: The Phi Kappa Phi Journal, 76*(1), Winter 1996. Copyright ©1996 by Diane DeNicola Orlofsky. By permission of the publishers.

David Labaree, Too easy a target: The trouble with ed schools and the implications for the university. *Academe, 85*(1). Washington, DC: American Association of University Professors, 1999. Reprinted by permission of the publisher. All rights reserved.

C. Madsen & T. Kuhn, *Contemporary Music Education*. Raleigh, NC: Contemporary Publishing Company of Raleigh, Inc., 1994. Reprinted by permission of the publisher. All rights reserved.

F. Maher & M. Tetreault, Knowledge versus pedagogy: The marginalization of teacher education. *Academe, 85*(1). Washington, DC: American Association of University Professors, 1999. Reprinted by permission of the publisher. All rights reserved.

Chapter One

Breaking the Mold

In "Communities of Learning and Thinking or a Context by Any Other Name," Ann Brown and Joseph Campione reported that while "Why can't Johnny read?" was a question often repeated in context with the American educational system of the 1970s, "Why can't Johnny think?" might indeed have replaced it as the question of choice for the 1980s.[1] Extend this line of questioning one step further, and we might arrive at another question, which has plagued many who trained future teachers during the 1990s and has continued to do so in the new millennium: "Why can't Johnny's teachers think?"

Where We Are

Let me build, from my vantage point as a teacher educator, a profile of the "typical" education student. Semester after semester, year after year, I teach young women and men who are polite, friendly, and eager to please. They attend class with acceptable regularity, make an effort to complete their assignments, and are generally personable and pleasant to be around. That is the "up" side of the equation. The downside is that most of them balk at the notion of creative approaches to problem solving. They respond with blank stares when faced with questions that attempt to extend their boundaries and comfort zones. They are too prone to compartmentalize and often can't (or won't) make the intuitive leaps necessary to apply previously acquired information to new tasks. The students come with very little vision for their own possibilities, much less for their future classrooms. They have a neat, sterile, safe image of what they think "teacher" means and are quite content to be mass-produced, carbon copies of that image. The students, however agreeable, are often one-dimensional, having little faith in their own potential and limited desire to explore new worlds and expand their own boundaries.

The most disturbing aspect is that most of these students fail to see how such a limited worldview and selfview will influence their success and effectiveness as teachers. They will, no doubt, also be quite content to manufacture little carbon copies of their tidy image of what a "student" should be, and the children who occupy their classrooms will endure the consequences.

Critics are quick to point the finger of indictment at the K–12 system for shallow preparation, or at the traditional teacher education system for perpetuating compartmentalization and emphasizing quantity over quality. Rhodes and Bellamy do not exaggerate when they assert that "on an almost daily basis, educators, policymakers, and the public call for reform or renewal of schools of education in general and initial teacher preparation in particular."[2] For example, Washington regularly heats up the teacher reform rhetoric. When researchers at the National Center for Education Statistics issued the report *Teacher Quality: A Report on the Preparation and Qualifications of Public School Teachers*, only one sound byte seemed to surface from the mind-numbing number of charts and graphs.[3] Less than half of the over 4,000 teachers polled indicated they felt prepared to teach upon college graduation. I'm sure this one piece of data stoked the fires of many critics of teacher education.

When Richard Riley, the Secretary of Education during the Clinton administration, referred to many Colleges of Education as "sleepy backwaters," I could almost hear critics of teacher education programs chant "a-ha-we-told-you-so" in perfect unison.[4] When teacher education becomes part of presidential and gubernatorial campaign trails and is caught in the ongoing culture war between left and right, we are often treated to laundry lists of new proposals with high price tags, regulatory programs, and flashy packaging of worn ideas.[5]

There have been plenty of reports within the last fifteen years that have been clarion calls for the reform of teacher education. Those of us employed as teacher educators are well aware of the information in the Holmes documents, the publication from the Carnegie Forum, reports from accrediting agencies and surveys from the Council for Basic Education and the Public Agenda, among others.[6] The authors of these publications identify a litany of deficiencies that they feel undermine the effectiveness of teacher education programs. Each indictment, whether it be fragmented curricula, inadequate school-based experiences, uninspired teaching methods, or out-of-touch professors, rings harsh and usually makes teacher educators wince and raise their defenses.

Personally, I have a great deal of respect for the work, effort, and conviction found in many of these documents, but I become frustrated when after every few years, the advocates of reform change course, and the profession is coerced into "reinventing the wheel" once again. National reform trends almost always filter down to individual institutions where policy shifts usually coincide with the latest state department of education or accrediting agency review. The accrediting agencies often view themselves as catalysts for reform, but it seems to me that far too many times Colleges of Education (or SCDEs as they are sometimes called) redefine themselves on paper in order to meet agency standards and maintain their accreditation status.[7] Reflection and change are periodically good for the soul of teacher education, but when an agency changes direction, SCDEs often try to make superheroic attempts to mold their working status into the agency's ideal. Many times the final results are uneven and don't truly reflect substantive, meaningful change. For example, we can theoretically assent to the content and message in the INTASC standards.[8] We can even go as far as to offically "adopt" them for our SCDEs. However, unless they translate into the daily realities of the teacher education classroom, the exercise is moot.

Accountability and rigorous self-examination are virtuous processes. Even so, I feel that what *really* matters in teacher education gets buried under bureaucratic red tape, administrative hoop-jumping, and endless reports filled with "educationese." Having labored over my fair share of these reports, I often make the comparison between myself and students who presume they can fake their way through an essay exam by giving me what they *think* I want to hear. Teacher education reform will not be advanced by the sheer exercise of thinking like the test-makers.

Accrediting agency standards, federal government initiatives, state departments of education licensing requirements, state government political agendas . . . it is enough to make any self-respecting teacher educator cry "Enough!" The authors of the teacher education reform literature rarely suggest ways in which the *individual teacher educator* can assist the process of reform because they themselves don't bridge the theory to practice gap. The reports tend to emphasize policy-making over people, focusing on the external superstructures of procedures, institutional flowcharts, labels, and gradient levels of achievement through testing. I contend that the essence of reform should be focused on the internal dynamics of teaching and learning within the microcosm of the teacher training classroom environment. Whereas the writers of these documents are astute and comprehensive in their analyses of the inherent weaknesses in the system and have significantly contributed to the national dialogue on teacher education, they are admittedly shortsighted when it comes to arriving at solutions and practical interventions.[9]

Enter the Higher Education Amendments (Title II) of 1998. Dovetailing this initiative into the work of the NCTAF (National Commission on Teaching and America's Future), the proposal authorizes grants to higher education institutions that partner with each other to create "lighthouse models of excellence" in teacher education and with high-poverty urban and rural school districts. Not surprisingly, Colleges of Education are scurrying to establish these partnerships in order to be eligible and competitive for the funds associated with Title II.[10] Never mind that their methods classrooms look and function the same. Never mind that their students are not encouraged to think critically and are rewarded for mediocrity. Teacher education is beginning to look like a movie set. Depending upon the plot, the props change. Even so, behind the scaffolding and drops, there lies a large, empty soundstage.

However, let's not waste time here pointing fingers at the drafters of reform documents. Negativity breeds negativity. To see for yourself how this can happen, read the "Whither Schools of Education" issue of the *Journal of Teacher Education*.[11] These words resonated in my head after reading Goodlad's lead article and the response articles: tension, isolation, marginalization, disdain, status deprivation, pessimism, congenital malaise. Such shrill rhetoric, innuendo, and wringing of hands are not productive. These kinds of exchanges may be meant to provoke discussion and provide catalysts for change, but they often degenerate to the verbal equivalent of a professional wrestling match.

What We Can Be

Let's focus, simplify, and issue a positive plan for change. *Teacher educators* should be held to a degree of accountability for their contributions to a field that is truly in need of reform. I contend that we need to redefine from within—one education classroom at a time. We are supposedly preparing young people to be dynamic, creative individuals who are ready for the realities of the teaching profession. We should make it our business to train individuals who won't be afraid to take risks, make transfers, search their value systems, hone their communication and management skills, and be models of competence in thinking and learning. However, we can teach this way only if we exhibit these traits in our own classroom pedagogy.

As a researcher, I am convinced of the efficacy of studying time-tested models in order to make application to current pedagogical situations. For example, when I wanted to establish operational definitions for quality teacher language behaviors as they should occur in the classroom, I studied the educational treatises of Roman orator Quintilian (ca. A.D. 35–95), Dutch humanist Desiderius Erasmus (ca. 1466–1536), and German philosopher and educator Johann Friedrich Herbart (1776–1841). The historical analysis yielded recurrent, and despite their separation in time, surprisingly similar positions on what is appropriate teacher language in the classroom. Out of theory came the development of a practical instructional language assessment instrument that can be used by both teacher educators and preservice educators to identify deficiencies in instructional language.[12] I now use this evaluation tool whenever I critique my students' lesson presentations. In my mind, this kind of process embodies the *essence* of action research.

It's no surprise, then, that I gravitated toward someone who historically has been a major force in educational theory to assist me in the exploration of better ways to train future teachers. Jerome S. Bruner is a name that truly needs no biographical tag to those of us in the fields of education and psychology. As Burton Welton reminds us, Jerome Bruner has "demonstrated an amazing capacity to invent new fields of study and to reinvent himself in the process. He has been a weathercock for the winds of change . . . ahead of the curve and leading the reformers."[13]

I first discovered Jerome S. Bruner during graduate school. One of my professors, the late Martha Harris Wurtz, handed me her copy of *The Process of Education* and said, "Go home, read, and report back tomorrow." She would often proudly say, "I am a Brunerian" as if being so associated her with an ethnic heritage or political affiliation. That incident began my twenty-year odyssey with Brunerian thought. From there, I read *Toward a Theory of Instruction, The Relevance of Education,* and *On Knowing: Essays for the Left Hand.* I applied Brunerian learning theories first to my public school students and eventually to my own college classroom.[14] However, with all due respect to Martha's memory, I have never called myself a Brunerian. I agree with Alison Gopnik's assessment that Bruner turns us into something "better than Brunerians. He turns [us] into [ourselves]."[15]

Over the years, I became convinced that the ideas set forth by Bruner were as relevant today as they were when they were written. More importantly, though, I began to initiate my own application of knowledge to the teacher education population. Even though Bruner initially targeted his learning theories toward children, I felt the need to revisit and implement those same theories to the young adults I was teaching. I began to reread as much Bruner as I could find, searching for areas that could be legitimately applied to the training of young adults—particularly those preparing to be teachers. After all, if we indeed tend to "teach as we are taught," then what better foundation to provide our future teachers than a curricular format and classroom environment grounded in Brunerian learning theories?

Bruner wrote that ". . . it is good practice [for students] to use their head to solve a problem by reflecting on what they already know or have learned. Are college students so different from fifth graders?"[16] After reading this statement, I felt justified in staying the course.

In 1994, I contacted Dr. Bruner in order to gain permission to access his private papers that are housed in the Harvard University Archives. I came away from the task convinced of the need in educational literature for a practical application of Bruner's principles to contemporary teacher training methodology. In the years since, I've discussed many things with Dr. Bruner, both in person and through correspondence. Because I believe in the relevance and timeliness of his ideas when applied to teacher education, I will spend the next few chapters revisiting Brunerian ideas on learning theory and pedagogy from the perspective of teacher training. I will also try to apply the theory to what I believe to be some of the *core* issues involved with teacher preparation (i.e., cultivation of mind, intuitive thinking, the relationship between learning and thinking, teaching for generalization and application, and communities of learners), while at the same time providing practical suggestions for the rejuvenation of daily life in teacher education classrooms. The reader will notice that I rely heavily on Bruner's writings as primary sources. Many of the scholars who have written about various aspects of Bruner's career were his former students, and I value their perspectives. However, I wanted to take a crack at shaping, what Bruner calls, my own *punta da vista*.[17]

In an issue of *Ethos,* Bradd Shore and Jerome Bruner let us in on an extended conversation that took place in 1996. At one point, Shore was musing about folks who spend years writing a book, afraid to release it from their grasp—uncertain of whether they've got it right. However, he reminds us, if we view writing as part of the "process of learning and meaning-making," then we are more likely to let it go, mistakes and all. Bruner added that it is also part of the process when someone responds to what you've written. They might even call you a damn fool, and you can respond in kind. It's a try and it is that "search for meaning" that keeps driving us, keeps pushing us to discover, make applications, delve deeper, and take chances. So, it seems time for me to enter the process, *punta da vista* in hand.[18]

I am well aware that the application of another's work is tricky business. Some would say irrelevant, others presumptuous. Bruner once told me that "I'm such a moving target that I'm a lousy candidate for a 'here's how it is' version [of my work]. And, personally, I'm more intrigued by what others make of my notions than what I think they REALLY mean. The life of the mind, after all, is lived in dialogue and now it's your turn."[19] So let me be clear. I am not using a cut-and-paste approach to Bruner's works to support my views. Nor am I claiming to have discovered a unique or revolutionary or superior or culturally more acceptable way to approach teacher training. Rather, my ideas represent an evolution—a series of reactions, applications, and counteradjustments, if you will—that grew out of twenty years of reading, studying, and appreciating Bruner's contributions to the literature.

I tread lightly and respectfully, knowing full well that "interpretation can never rise above or escape from the situation of interpretation it seeks to interpret even when it is hidden behind the mask of explanation."[20] I have tried to gingerly maneuver around the quicksand of oversimplification throughout this book, while realizing that the nature and scope of an overview of this magnitude makes the task of maintaining context and perspective difficult, at best. I offer Bruner's written musings on these subjects as a catalyst to spur on our own musings, to redirect our thoughts, to enliven our inner dialogues. I also understand that narratives are often constructed with the audience rhetorically in mind and that each one reflects its own version of the intellectual landscape. I relate this narrative as much to myself as to those teacher educators who choose to come along for the ride.

During a lecture to science educators in 1992, Bruner said that "we need a surer sense of what to teach to whom and how to go about teaching it in such a way that it will make those taught more effective, less alienated, and better human beings."[21] With that educational challenge, we begin.

Notes

1. A. L. Brown & J. C. Campione. (1990). Communities of learning and thinking, or a context by any other name. In D. Kuhn (Ed.), *Developmental perspectives on teaching and learning thinking skills* (pp. 108–126). Basel: Karger.

2. L. K. Rhodes & G. T. Bellamy. (1999). Choices and consequences in the renewal of teacher education. *Journal of Teacher Education, 50*, 17.

3. L. Lewis, E. Farris, B. Parsad, N. Carey, B. Smerdon, N. Bartfai, Westat, Pelavin Research Center, & American Institutes for Research. (1999, January). *Teacher quality: A report on the preparation and qualifications of public school teachers.* Retrieved May 5, 2000, from the World Wide Web: www.nces.ed.gov/pub99/1999080.html.

4. R. W. Riley. (1999, February). *New challenges, a new resolve: Moving American education into the 21st century.* Sixth annual State of American Education speech, Long Beach, CA.

5. At the writing of this book, the presidential race was between George W. Bush and Albert Gore. Gore had just proposed creating a "21st-century Teachers Corps" and offered to provide signing bonuses for professionals who switched careers to teach. Retrieved May 5, 2000, from the World Wide Web: www.cnn.com/2000/allpolitics/stories/05/05/gore.education/index.html.

6. The Holmes trilogy includes *Tomorrow's teachers* (1986), *Tomorrow's schools* (1990), and *Tomorrow's schools of education* (1995). The Carnegie Forum's report is titled *A nation prepared: Teachers for the 21st century* (1986). Other applicable reports include S. Farkas & J. Johnson. (1997). *Different drummers: How teachers of teachers view public education.* New York: The Public Agenda; D. W. Rigden. (1996). *What teachers have to say about teacher education.* Washington, DC: Council for Basic Education; National Commission on Teaching and America's Future. (1996). *What matters most: Teaching for America's future.* New York: Author.

7. A. E. Wise. (2000). Performance-based accreditation: Reform in action. *The Newsletter of the National Council for Accreditation of Teacher Education, 9*(2), 1–2.

8. INTASC stands for Interstate New Teacher Assessment and Support Consortium. These core standards may be found on the website of the Council of Chief State School Officers (CCSSO) at: www.ccsso.org/intascst.html

9. For an excellent analysis of the Holmes initiative, read *The rise and stall of teacher education reform* by Michael Fullan, Gary Galluzzo, Patricia Morris, and Nancy Watson (AACTE Publications, 1998). For a thorough overview and analysis of reports from the Carnegie Forum, the Holmes Group, the Center for Edu-

cational Renewal, the National Commission for Excellence in Teacher Education, the National Council for the Accreditation of Teacher Education, Project 30 Alliance, the Renaissance Group, the Teacher Education Initiative, and the Teacher Education Accreditation Council, see the following article: L. Valli & P. L. Rennert-Arriev. (2000). Identifying consensus in teacher education reform documents: A proposed framework and action implications. *Journal of Teacher Education, 51*(1), 5–17. For an individual's perspective on criticism of teacher education programs, see: D. C. Berliner. (2000). A personal response to those who bash teacher education. *Journal of Teacher Education, 51*(5), 358–371.

10. For information regarding Teacher Quality Enhancement Grants and Partnership Grants, use the following website: www.ed.gov/inits/teachers/index.html.

11. This issue of the *Journal of Teacher Education* is Volume 50(5).

12. D. N. DeNicola. (1986). The development of an instructional language assessment instrument based upon the historical perspectives of Quintilian, Erasmus, and Herbart and its use in analyzing the language behaviors of preservice elementary and music education majors. (Doctoral dissertation, Florida State University, 1986). *Dissertation Abstracts International, 47*, 08A.

13. For a concise and thorough overview of Bruner's contributions and evolutions, see B. Welton. (1999). The message and the medium: The roots/routes of Jerome Bruner's Postmodernism. *Theory and Research in Social Education, 27*(2), 169–178.

14. Examples of resulting papers include: The effect of sequential instruction upon elementary education majors' ability to match pitch and perform prescribed song-leading tasks. *PMEA Bulletin of Research in Music Education, 19*, 23–33 (co-authored with Nancy Barry); and, *The development and evaluation of a twelve-step sequential method to teach class piano sightreading.* Paper presented to the Music Educators National Conference Southern Division Convention, Winston-Salem, NC, 1990.

15. A. Gopnik. (1990). Knowing, doing and talking: The Oxford years. *Human Development, 33*, 338.

16. J. S. Bruner. (1971). *The relevance of education.* New York: W.W. Norton and Company, 74.

17. J. Bruner (personal communication, June 22, 2000).

18. B. Shore. (1997). Keeping the conversation going: An interview with Jerome Bruner. *Ethos, 25*(1), 13.

19. J. Bruner (personal communication, October 14, 1996).

20. J. S. Bruner. (1993). Explaining and interpreting: Two ways of using the mind. In G. Harman (Ed.), *Conceptions of the mind: Essays in honor of George A. Miller* (pp. 123–137). Hillsdale, NJ: Lawrence Erlbaum Associates, 129.

21. J. S. Bruner. (1992, March). Science education and teachers: A Karplus lecture. *Journal of Science Education and Technology, 1*(1), 6.

Bruner On . . .

Head Start

Most of us "get good at" one or two things in the course of a lifetime. Jerome Bruner seems to "get good at" most anything upon which he sets his sights. Whether analyzing World War II communiques, sailing across the Atlantic, pioneering efforts in infant research, or taking a hard look at poverty in America, Bruner excelled with zest and vision.[1]

Without a doubt, those who know Bruner know he is a wonderful storyteller with intriguing stories to tell. I have chosen a few that will, I hope, appeal to teacher educators or anyone who is interested in educational issues. Each story will be a narrative "island," of sorts, placed between the chapters of this book.

The first such island gives a glimpse into the merger of politics, policy, program, and philosophy in the form of Head Start. In 1995, Bruner told me about his involvement in the conception of Head Start. It's a great story—a fascinating piece of history that continues to impact lives today. According to FY1998 figures, 820,000 children were enrolled in Head Start. Thirteen percent of those children (ages 3–5) were diagnosed with an exceptionality of some kind. The spin-off Early Head Start program began in 1994 and, according to FY1998 statistics, served 35,000 children under the age of three. Government data reveal that 55% of participating families in FY1998 earned incomes less than $9,000 per year; 73% made less than $12,000.[2] Here is an excerpt of Bruner's own account of the remarkable birth of Head Start:

> At the same time, in America, there developed a new movement toward greater consciousness with respect to race [and] class, which is symbolized by the great decision of Brown that desegregated our schools and made people aware of the

fact that there [was] something more than just strict middle-class values. Public conscientiousness was very much aroused by that, and people began to believe increasingly that Head Start was a wonderful idea.

I suppose I have a sudden *parti pris* in that I was one of the people who proposed it, and that itself was a fantastic story.[3]

* * * * *

[A] good friend, Adam Yarmolinsky, a brilliant young lawyer and one of Robert MacNamara's "whiz kids," had just become Sargent Shriver's principal aide in the new Office of Economic Opportunity, established by President Johnson to lead the "war on poverty." When I told Yarmolinsky about the currently circulating ideas for something like a "head start" for deprived children, he arranged for me to see Shriver, whose wife and I had served together on the Board of the John F. Kennedy Center in Nashville. I broached the idea. Shriver's response was: "Are you *seriously* proposing that the *federal* government get into nursery schools when we hardly dare to poke a nose into ordinary public education in the States? It's political dynamite." I departed for the Boston plane.

About a week later, at cocktails before dinner, the phone rang. It was Shriver asking if I could come down to talk more about "that idea." The conversation was curious the next day. I had mentioned "pilot projects" to explore how such a program might be put together, having very much in mind the models that had been tried out by Susan Gray and Nick Hobbis in Tennessee and by Bettye Caldwell in Syracuse.

Shriver was urging that in a matter as important as this one, pilot projects were "too fastidious." If the need is there, one plunges in. In the American political perspective of that time, I suspect he was right. So Head Start came into being.[4]

* * * * *

But never underrate the power of antinomies to work themselves into public consciousness. By the early 1970s, research began "proving" that IQ gains from Head Start disappeared within a few years, and, even federal financing of Head Start was questioned, in this new period of urban austerity. It did not disappear, but neither did it grow as much as it might have. It survived because it had created a new consciousness that by intervening in the developmental scene early enough, you could change the life of children later. I say this was a "faith," for during those years, there was not much direct evidence that Head Start had "permanent" effects (or that it didn't). Ironically, when the twenty-five-year results on Head Start began coming in, they showed that it had made an astonishing difference, even if it hadn't produced a mass miracle. . . . Kids who had been through it were, by comparison to "controls," more likely to stay longer and do better in school, to get and to hold jobs longer, to stay out of jail, to commit fewer crimes. It "paid": the cost per pupil far offset economic losses from unemployment, cost of imprisonment, and welfare payments. It was "good for the society" in hard-nosed socioeconomic terms, even if it didn't turn the trick for each individual child.[5]

* * * * *

Fortunately, Head Start survives, and it may take many years before such an institution takes a shape suitable to its task.[6]

Notes

1. The bibliography for this book is divided into two sections. The first gives a partial listing of Bruner's written contributions that may be of interest to teacher educators and educators. These include the works I have cited throughout the manuscript in addition to others. The second part lists selected secondary sources that were useful in the writing of this book.

2. For current statistics on Head Start, see: www2.acf.dhhs.gov/programs/hsb/faq.htm.

3. J. S. Bruner. (1996). What we have learned about early learning. *European Early Childhood Education Research Journal, 4*(1), 11.

4. J. S. Bruner. (1980). Jerome S. Bruner. In G. Lindzey (Ed.), *History of psychology in autobiography*, Vol. 7 (pp. 75–151). San Francisco: W. H. Freeman, 136.

5. J. S. Bruner. What we have learned about early learning, 11.

6. J. S. Bruner. Jerome S. Bruner, 137.

Chapter Two

Leaping the Barrier

I had a colleague whose primary class assignment involved Foundations of Education courses. He was an educator who genuinely felt that it was his responsibility to encourage students to answer the question *why?* He urged introspection as to the reasons they chose the profession and then demanded intellectualization of their answers. He wanted students to ask the *right* questions, not to parrot the *right* responses.[1] Environments such as these have a genuine purpose within the educational core curriculum, and I applaud the efforts of educators who begin the preparatory process in a rigorous manner. Unfortunately, I have witnessed too many introductory courses that only serve to offer generalizations, educational clichés, and theoretical niceties that, at best, merely rake the surface of the students' minds.

I sometimes view the minds of my preservice students as *soil*. General education classes (such as "Foundations of Education" courses) have the *potential* to be experiences where the soil of the students' minds is tilled. To be truly effective, these courses should seize the opportunity to rototill the soil, overturning large chunks in order to prepare the mind for what is to follow.

For discussion purposes in this text, however, methods classes that have as their core a particular subject specialty (such as mathematics education, children's literature, music education, and so on) will be referred to most often. These classes allow a merger between content and methodology, and provide the instructor with opportunities to both plant the seeds of a particular discipline while fertilizing, weeding, and further preparing the soil. Meaningful, practical teaching experiences will reveal the results of the planting efforts with the yield of the harvest occurring during the first year of teaching and beyond. Also note that throughout this book, any attempts to wed theory to practice are done cautiously, knowing full well that "attempts to specify the route from what teachers can or should do—teach, mentor, monitor, and criticize—to what children do—think and learn, remember, generalize—make up a long and less than satisfactory story."[2]

To Think . . . to Learn . . . Perchance, to Dream

One of our greatest challenges involves students' awareness of the vital connection, a life-defining link, if you will, between learning and thinking. One might imagine that a young adult who has chosen education as a life profession would be intimately acquainted with this union. Too often, however, my education majors opt for the easier classes where they will be spoon-fed. When they are "forced" to reach deep for a response, make generalizations, or provide creative solutions, they either freeze and balk, or cut and run:

> . . . Learning something in a generic way is like leaping over a barrier. On the other side of the barrier is thinking. When the generic has been grasped, it is then that we are able to recognize the new problems we encounter as exemplars of old principles we have mastered. . . . Thinking is the reward for learning and we may be systematically depriving our students of this reward as far as school learning is concerned.[3]

In *The Relevance of Education*, Bruner further explored the links between learning and thinking: "There is nothing more central to a discipline than its way of thinking. There is nothing more important than to provide the child [or student] the earliest opportunity to learn that way of thinking—the forms of connection, the attitudes, hopes, jokes, and frustrations that go with it."[4]

After reading the address Bruner delivered in 1992 at the Karplus science education lecture series, I was struck by one of his statements. He suggested that not only should we as teachers be working on ways to pose challenging questions, but we should endeavor to cultivate such questions and attempt to keep them alive simply because they are *good* questions and worthy of further thought. I began to reflect on this idea in order to find a way to make the practical link between Bruner's provocative idea and the methods classroom. So one semester, in an effort to keep good questions alive, I asked the students to keep journals. I told them to explore the questions that might have been raised in classroom discussions or that were currently part of their repertoire of concerns. After sixteen entries, I collected the journals. I'm not sure what I expected, but it definitely was *not* what I received. Many responded literally and took questions that had been raised in this and other education classes, heading each entry with a different question. I didn't even mind that the format was predictable, but what I was not prepared for was the shallowness of the responses. Many gave pat, clichéd answers that were unimaginative, banal, and, above all, safe. I could predict with alarming accuracy their simplistic views on everything from "should students wear school uniforms?" to "the use of teacher testing."

Rarely did I get a glimpse at someone's passionate feelings regarding an issue or even at how their minds worked as they allowed themselves the luxury of pondering, even meditating on questions that were worth the mental exercise. I shared with them one of the last statements of Bruner's Karplus lecture: "One of the great triumphs of learning (and of teaching) is to get things organized in your head in a way that permits you to know more than you 'ought to.' And this takes reflection, brooding about what it is that you know. The enemy of reflection is the breakneck pace—the thousand pictures."[5] I implored them to dig deeper for the next sixteen entries, promising support, confidentiality, and open-mindedness regardless of the material within the journals.

The next round of entries showed little improvement. I remember communicating my disappointment over the results of this simple pedagogical experiment to Dr. Bruner. His response was rhetorical—Why *is* it so hard to put *any* pedagogical ideas into practice? He mused that "the thing about keeping good questions alive is that, God willing, they may keep some people awake. I find myself increasingly of the view that it is as much a state of somnambulism that is destroying our contemporary American scene as it is hostility." He also encouraged me to change the format, to try shaking up the question by raising the stakes. He suggested using another genre other than journals to record the questions they want to keep alive. Bruner reasoned that most people, given a dilemma such as "If you knew you were going to die next week and had a last question you'd like answered (aside from "Why me?), what would it be?" would jump at the chance to intellectualize the question. Can most preservice educators think abstractly and symbolically enough to reach the spirit of the exercise as Bruner intended? I contend that until the barrier between learning and thinking is scaled, their attempts will continue to miss the mark.[6]

Just how has the link between learning and thinking become interrupted, and in many of the students' lives, become completely separate entities that rarely, if ever, converge? Unfortunately, I believe that we in educational circles have contributed to this separation in several ways:

1. by emphasizing breadth of coverage over depth;
2. by deemphasizing the use of intuitive thinking;
3. by relying and placing great emphasis upon extrinsic reward as the sole motivator for continued attempts at learning.

Education Is Not a Quiz Show

Bruner lamented the tendency of educational institutions to emphasize extensive coverage of material over that of intensive and thorough examination. Once he even described this inclination as an "epistemological mystery."[7] In an autobiographical sketch that I discovered in archival research, Bruner recounted that subject matter penetration was the education ideal at Woods Hole. The famous conference publicly carried this banner, in the face of those frantic educators who feared our students weren't getting *enough* material.[8]

There seems to be general affirmation that the best learning environment is one that allows for more than just a cursory examination of the subject at hand. Nevertheless, so many of us in teacher preparation feel constrained by the clock, or fiscal year divisions, or state requirements, or a host of other external motivators. We rarely allow our classrooms to be centers for reflection, for debate, for making connections, or for conjecture. We end up compartmentalizing our subject and end up *talking* about the subject rather than *doing* the subject. This has a double-edged effect because our students will no doubt model their classroom approach on ours. If this is indeed the case, then every methods class should strive to be a pedagogical model.

> It was basically this set of convictions that led those of us who were in the midst of curriculum reform to propose that *doing* physics is what physics instruction should be about—even if the instruction had a very limited coverage. And we proposed that doing it from the start was necessary, even if at the outset the student had only the vaguest intuition to fall back upon. The basic objective was to make the subject your own, to make it part of your own thinking—whether physics, history, ways of looking at painting or whatnot. There follows from this view of competence as the objective of education some rather firm conclusions about educational practice.[9]

The notion of *doing* the subject before you really *know* the subject is not only pedagogically sound advice, but it is deeply rooted in human reflex maneuvers. Infants and toddlers experience and do first, then label and learn cause and effect later. As toddlers, my daughters made up their own words to accompany pictures in a book without knowing that they were experimenting with word substitution and narrative. The girls were also fully responsive to the music they heard, making up little dances and moving rather accurately to the beat without any realization that there was a distinct difference between beat and rhythm. The factual knowledge they gained later was internalized much more readily because they had actually experienced the concept first.

For example, to introduce and illustrate the concept of beat and rhythm for students and the broader concept of doing the subject prior to processing all the facts, I assemble a tape montage of song excerpts. At the beginning of the tape, the students encounter popular tunes to which they almost instinctively respond to the beat by foot tapping. The first three pieces, although they represent vastly different popular genres (pop, country, rock), all have the same beat definition and tempi. I stop the tape after the three excerpts and ask if their foot movements changed in any way between pieces. After they reply that the movements did not alter, we go on to hear other types of music. As the tape progresses, the beat often is obscured, and it becomes a challenge to locate it. I also have the students respond with arm swaying so that they can experience division of the beat. I label and define beat, rhythm, tempo, and meter only *after* this hands-on episode. The concepts become much less abstract and further explanations become clearer as a result. Granted, proceeding directly to the conceptual definitions without the tape would on the surface seem to save class time. Uultimately though, without this experience, additional time would be needed to redefine and clarify the concept. Doing without all the facts is not only possible, it is vital.

My advice? Every so often, forget about the clock. Take an additional class period to expand upon an idea, pursue other discussion options, muse on the "but-what-ifs." For example, after discussing *1001 Nights*, my husband (who is an English professor) often feels pressed to move on to Chaucer. Even so, he takes additional instructional time to get the students to construct their own version of the 1002nd night. He gives them certain character and plot devices such as a lost merchant, a flying carpet, a pot of gold, a talking dog, an oasis, a dark-eyed princess. The students then have to incorporate as many devices as possible while maintaining the spirit of the original 14th-century Arabic stories. In doing this creative extension of the original work, the students should demonstrate Scheherazade's strategy in her storytelling. Every night, Scheherazade stops her tale at the climax to whet the King's appetite as to the tale's conclusion; in doing so, she keeps herself alive for another day. My husband's admonition to the students—"Don't lose your head!"

If we value learning and thinking and see the need to help our students leap between the two, perhaps we should reexamine our bondage to the hands of the clock. As Bruner reminds us:

> It matters not what we have learned. What we can do with what we have learned, this is the issue. . . . Let us not judge our students simply on what they know. That is the philosophy of the quiz program. Rather, let them be judged on what they can generate from what they know—how well they can leap the barrier from learning to thinking.[10]

The Virtue of Intuition

> . . . it is quite plain that learning and teaching must start from some intuitive level. This may be true not only of young children entering the educational establishment for the first time, but of anybody approaching a new body of knowledge or skills for the first time.[11]

Look up the word *intuition* in your favorite dictionary. I guarantee that the formal definition will leave you perplexed as to how intuitive thinking encourages the leap between learning and thinking. Bruner has spent a great deal of effort extolling the virtues of intuition and its place in educational circles, so I turned to his writings for a clearer grasp of intuition, analysis, and their codependent natures.

A more distinct picture might be drawn if a synopsis (Figure 1) was used in place of ordinary dictionary definitions. The chart summarizes the characteristics of analytical and intuitive thinking as they are discussed by Bruner throughout many of his writings.[12] As a preface to this and other capsulizations found within this book, I must admit that my penchant to summarize vast amounts of information in chart or diagram form seems to be a manifestation of the analytical side of my nature. However, I would *prefer* to think of it as just another application of a principle suggested by Bruner: If you want to simplify, climb on your own shoulders, look down at what you just did (or read) and see if you can represent it back to yourself in some form.[13] I guess I feel justified by Bruner's words:

> There are ways for using the mind in a fashion designed to save work, to make seemingly difficult problems easier, to bring a complicated matter into the range of one's attention. One rarely speaks of them, and sure there are no courses for teaching them. One learns to make little diagrams or to use a matrix.[14]

Traditionally, classrooms have tended to emphasize analytical forms of thinking. According to Bruner, young children often risk losing the very

Characteristics of Analytical and Intuitive Thinking

ANALYTICAL	INTUITIVE
One step at a time	Grasps meaning, significance, structure of a problem, apart from reliance upon analytical properties
Steps are explicit	Basic familiarity with knowledge involved
Steps can be explained, communicated, reported	Often difficult to communicate how answer was derived
Gives problems a form	Invents or discovers problems
Sequences steps in linear order	Intuitive facility increases with emphasis on structures; connectedness of knowledge
Step-by-step inductive process plus experimentation plus research design plus statistical analysis	Not necessary to be aware of the process in order to arrive at an answer; aware of incompleteness, need to investigate further
Focuses on parts	Focuses on the whole
Requires a formulated structural sense of the problem	Precedes proof; sense of wrongness or rightness
Application of analytical principles increases confidence	Fostered by each student's level of self-confidence

Figure 1. Comparison of Analytical and Intuitive Thought Processes

intuitive sense by which they have previously solved problems once they enter the formalized classroom. Intuition often gets dampened down and may even go underground. An inservice second-grade teacher once told me that when kids enter kindergarten, they have a special spark in their eyes; the one that reveals curiosity, eagerness, intuitive reasoning, and enthusiasm for learning. She sadly related that by the time they reached her, the spark had almost entirely disappeared.

My husband relates a story that further illustrates this point. He recalls that in fourth grade his class was assigned an art project with toothpicks and glue. Most of the kids made stick figures, houses, or other representational objects. He chose to make a geometric, three-dimensional figure. His teacher's reaction? Dismay. When the artwork was displayed, his product was shoved toward the back, as if to hide his contribution. His nine-year-old mind was experimenting with shapes, designs, and abstract forms, but it was unappreciated by the very person who should have been encouraging its production—the teacher.

Bruner said that a balanced education enables a child to "proceed intuitively when necessary and to analyze when appropriate."[15] And what about preservice teacher educators? Do they have a concept of intuition and its place in their own intellectual lives and in the lives of their future students? In my experience, they do not. They crave the analytical approach to problem solving; better yet, they approach learning as a give-and-take proposition. They want the methods teacher to give them all the information that they need to stay one step ahead of the children. They, in turn, will learn all the facts, including little thumbnail sketches of child development stages and skill hierarchies and give back their knowledge to you on examinations. They believe this system will adequately prepare them for the teaching field.

For example, I recently had a graduate student ask me for help with a paper for another class. He had been assigned Bruner and his instructor, knowing of my work on this book, told him to come and "pick my brain." Now, I am always quite happy to enter into dialogue with students about Bruner. However, I was not prepared for this exchange. He said, "So, what can you tell me about Bruner?" Incredulous, I responded with "What have you found?" He retrieved several summaries (pathetic ones, at that) downloaded from the World Wide Web, which he had *not* read. I pointed to a shelf filled with notes, manuscript revisions . . . in essence, 20 years of research. I then lifted a two-inch thick document that was Dr. Bruner's partial list of publications since 1939. I told him to go and read and *then* come back. I would be more than happy to discuss it then but would not provide him with convenient, pedantic sound bytes. He never returned.

This kind of intellectual inertia in our preservice population alarms me. Where is the realization that they will be dealing with classrooms full of individuals who bring their own unique learning styles and varying life experiences to the learning arena? Where is the understanding that they need to cultivate the seeds of intuitive thought in their *own* studies in order to prepare them to create a classroom atmosphere where intuition is cherished, not punished? When I deal with in-service teachers at conventions or meetings, they usually want me (as clinician) to provide them with 101 workable ideas that can be implemented Monday morning at 8:00 a.m. I must admit, I craved quick fixes when I taught public school, too. The sheer frantic pace of the life of a teacher often contributes to this thirst for practical, easily implemented, GREAT ideas.

So, how should the methods teacher help education students shake off intuitive inertia? First of all, by personally providing an intuitive model for them to follow. *We need to be willing to guess and then to subject these guesses to critical analysis.* Many academicians feel uncomfortable with this mode of thinking, but a firm grasp of the structure of a specific subject and all the ways in which it connects with other areas can increase our ease with intuitive thinking.[16] Bruner reminded us that we, as teachers, should be working models of intuitive thinking. We should not demand or expect that the students necessarily emulate our model, but if they respect us, they will often want to make our standards their own.[17]

Next, we need to provide an environment that not only encourages intuitive responses, but seeks to protect and defend them provided that they lead to further inquiry. For those who question the focus of such inquiries, remember that intuition does *not* have to be vague—it *should* lead to further digging as "intuition is an invitation to go further—whether intuitively or analytically."[18]

Listen to this remarkably charged atmosphere Bruner described:

> If the teacher wishes to close down the process of wondering by flat declarations of fixed factuality, he or she can do so. The teacher can also open wide a topic of [locution] to speculation and negotiation. To the extent that the materials of education are chosen for their amenableness to imaginative transformation and are presented in a light to invite negotiation and speculation, to that extent education becomes a part of what I earlier called "culture making." The pupil, in effect, becomes a party to the negotiatory process by which facts are created and interpreted. He becomes at once an agent of knowledge making as well as a recipient of knowledge transmission.[19]

What if *every* classroom contained elements of this interplay between intuition and analysis? In practice, this kind of dynamic would revolutionize how we conduct the day-to-day educational affairs in the classroom. So we need to ask ourselves this question: "What would this type of environment look like in a college education methods class?"

I believe that in order to provide an intuition-friendly environment, the current system needs a four-fold overhaul:

1. change the integrity of daily classroom dialogue;
2. alter the structure of assignments and examinations;
3. create room and opportunity for guessing;
4. modify the external reward system.

Dynamic Dialogues

> Entering the culture is perhaps most readily done by entering a dialogue with a more experienced member of it. Perhaps one way in which we might reconsider the issue of teacher training is to give the teacher training in the skills of dialogue—how to discuss a subject with a beginner. There are doubtless many ways in which a human being can serve as a vicar of the culture, helping a child to understand its points of view and the nature of its knowledge. But I dare say that few are so potentially powerful as participating in dialogue.[20]

A fairly obvious way to influence the quality of classroom dialogue is to focus on appropriate questioning techniques. The methods instructor needs to cultivate the art of asking good questions—questions that require a thoughtful response, not a one-word factual retort. The questioning process (and the layering of questions) can be one way to encourage the leap between learning and thinking. What happens when no answers are forthcoming? My usual approach is to wait, perhaps rephrasing the question (without revealing additional information). If there is still no response, I tell them that they know where to find the answers, or at least in what general direction to begin, and that we will return to the question the next day. Isn't this the whole idea behind Bloom's Cognitive Domain Taxonomy? It is my effort to increase the level of intellectual thought and discourse, to demand higher-order thinking. This approach is also consistent with my philosophy of "spoon-feeding-stops-here." Frankly, I am tired of education classes having the reputation of being pushover classes for the thought-impaired student who can't handle a more "difficult" major. We need to fight these misconceptions by demanding that our students think for themselves. Even when asked a common question such as "How many pages does the paper have to be?" my typical response is "As many as it needs to be to achieve your goal." This answer often infuriates some students, but I follow it with a statement like "Many of you will be teaching in a matter of months. If your principal asks you for a written report, will your first response to his request be *how many pages does it have to be?*"

This brings up the issue of accountability. Bruner took a three-month leave of absence to teach a class of fifth-graders. He shared that "the quality of thought in those seminars was unbelievable, after the children accepted the idea of accountability for their own utterances."[21] They came to realize that there had to be substance behind their thoughts and utterances plus the ability to provide explanations.

Methods instructors should also urge their students to be accountable for classroom contributions. More often than I like to admit, I have probed further into a student's comment, only to realize that there was nothing substantive behind it . . . merely words for words' sake. If we allow our students to spout unchallenged clichés, then we perpetuate the notion that education students are shallow-minded, insipid clones of inept, out-of-touch instructors. There are some hard questions to be asked and answered in educational arenas today—there is no room for ignorance, complacency, false piety, passivity, or the undisciplined mind.

The area of accountability also should extend to the areas of professionalism and integrity. Students should begin to examine their words with an eye toward how they will function for those individuals seated around them. Our society's discourse is full of negatives. Just think of how we give simple commands: "Don't slam the door," "Don't put that there." Rewording these statements in the positive ("Please close the door quietly," "Let me show you where that goes") takes little effort and is much more edifying and uplifting. I believe we have to start sensitizing our future teachers to the power of their verbal communication. Words can either hurt or heal, and as teachers, they will be wielding great power by their word choices.

We also need to address issues such as intent versus function. At some point in our lives, we have all said "Oh, I didn't mean it that way." However, the point of argument was mute because what we said functioned for the hearer in a way different from how it was intended. Sarcasm is a wonderful example of intent/function abuse. A teacher may intend for a sarcastic remark to be amusing, but many times it functions in a hurtful way for the student on the receiving end. Set up daily dialogue in the methods classroom so that it reflects what the model classroom should be—full of support, positive encouragement, acceptance, and constructive critiques.

Students need to realize that they are all in this learning process *together*. According to Bruner, students usually assume that teachers have all the knowledge and that we pass it on to the class. All things being equal, they should soon discover that others have knowledge to share as well. Group discussion can be a way of creating knowledge rather than merely seeing who has it. If nobody in the group knows the answer, "leaping into culture as a warehouse, a toolhouse" into the heads of more knowledgeable people can be the route.[22] I first heard the phrase "community of learners" from Dr. Bruner. He related an anecdote about an elementary classroom in Oakland, California, where the teacher, Ann Brown, presented the problem of how to clean up the *Exxon Valdez* spill, particularly when it came to the removal of oil from the animals involved.

After much discussion, the kids decided that some kind of oil blotter should be used, but the problem was how to find one that was large enough to accommodate all the oil. One youngster mentioned that peanut butter would be a good choice. When pressed further for a reason, he categorically responded that everyone knows that when you open up a jar of peanut butter, you see oil on the top. Another long deliberation ensued regarding acquisition and transport of all the jars of peanut butter to the site. A class stenographer recorded the proceedings so that the class had a written record of how they collectively worked to solve the problem. With teacher as facilitator, the class demonstrated collaborative learning at its best, with writing, transferring, communicating, tallying, debating, listening, and logic skills being exercised. The students learned to elicit information from each other's pre-existent pool of knowledge, realizing the ultimate good that resulted from scaffolding on each other's ideas.[23]

Bruner also recalled the "Chicago anecdote" in one of his articles. Here, the children were given a map of the central states in which only rivers and large bodies of water, agricultural products, and natural resources were identified. They were not allowed to consult textbooks, but they had to use what knowledge the group brought to the task to try and find out where Chicago might be on the map. After forty-five minutes and some very perceptive guesses, Chicago was not located—but that no longer mattered because the children had been exercising the exciting elements of induction, deduction, reasoning, logic, and analogy along with developing a sense of appreciation for the ideas of others, tolerance, and a host of desirable attributes. The facts could and would come later as well as an appreciation for the work of other more knowledgeable "learners."[24]

An episode I recall from my graduate school days further illustrates the need for students to leap the hurdles between learning and thinking and highlights the role of teacher as facilitator in the process. I wrote about this event in a piece for *Proteus* titled "In Memoriam," and repeat an excerpt here to illustrate the point:

"Learning is, most often, figuring out how to use what you already know in order to go beyond what you currently think."[25]

I can still hear her voice, raspy from too many cigarettes and years of delivering lectures.

"Diane, I want you to find this 13th-century manuscript, and you have three days in which to accomplish your task."

She yielded nothing more by way of instruction—no detailed directions were given. So for three days, I bumped into and plowed through manuscript collections such as the *Magnus liber organi*, reproductions of the Wolfenbüttel 677 and 1206, and many other volumes of early music that seemed to lead me no closer to the elusive manuscript. I had paused along the way to absorb an interesting fact or an obscure conjecture, but felt as if I were spiraling down through a funnel. I could only hope that the manuscript lay at the narrow end of my search. It did not.

Three days later, I faced the inevitable.

"So, what have you found?" she asked.

"Nothing," I replied. "I couldn't locate the manuscript."

My words seemed to mingle with the smoke in the room. She pushed away from the desk, leaned her large-boned frame back in the chair, and took a long drag from her half-spent cigarette.

"That is because the manuscript does not exist."

Each word seemed italicized by the puffs of smoke that accompanied it. Few times during my graduate studies had I ever been at a loss for words, but this definitely qualified as one of those times.

I think I muttered, "I don't understand."

She began to speak crisply and formally, as was her manner.

"Now, sit down and tell me everything you discovered in your search. What sources did you use that had been previously unfamiliar to you? What deduction processes did you utilize? Tell me everything. Her unruly, grey-flecked eyebrows lifted in expectation, as if to say, "Well?"

This must be some cruel joke, I thought. Three days of exhaustive research for an imaginary manuscript? I remember plopping into the chair and retrieving my notes from a worn canvas bag. The familiarity of the bag was somehow comforting as I haltingly told her of my adventure. I had no idea that this exercise, although unconventional, had in no small way prepared me for all sorts of searches to come.[26]

A teacher pushed me past my comfort zone and the experience served to uncover my intuitive skills. Each success makes the next leap easier and less intimidating—and isn't that part of why we teach?

Evaluating the Evaluations

The structure of our assignments and examinations also needs to be re-examined in order to maximize their capacity to propel the students into both intuitive and analytical thinking. At the root of this discussion lies the issue of effort—ours, not theirs. I am not advocating the total abandonment of the scantron test, as long as the questions challenge the students' grasp of the issues and not just the facts. Substituting probing dialectics and analogues for the "names and dates" format will require a much greater effort on our behalf (in terms of test construction and evaluation), but I believe it might yield greater learning outcomes. Instead of designing a "who-did-what-when" question for *Antigone*, design a question along the lines of "Based on your reading of *Antigone*, examine a situation where you were faced with a similar predicament." The subtext here would be that students understand the dilemma of allegiance to the laws of the gods or one's conscience in contrast to the laws of the state and make applications to their own life experiences.

Competency-based assignments are useful in classes where a physical skill is being taught. For example, when I teach a class in which the students have to demonstrate their proficiency on an instrument (as one of many course requirements), I often make the periodic skill tests competency-based. The students know the skill that will be checked, and they have a window of opportunity, if you will, to pass off the skill. Competency might be set at 80% (different percentages for the difficulty level of the skill involved) and if competency is met, they can move on to the next skill. Failure to reach competence means that they have to stay with that skill until they can reach the appropriate rate of competency. The structure of the assignment and ensuing examination of the skill allows the students to focus on the task and makes them more sensitive to their rate of progress.

Other assignments are specifically designed to force the students to pull from the knowledge bases they already possess and creatively apply them to a new area. The population of my elementary music methods classes consists of elementary, early childhood, and special education majors. One assignment that met with success involved the development of an across-the-curriculum teaching unit. The class was instructed to choose a children's literature book appropriate to their target population. Then they were required to find three age-appropriate children's songs that correlated with the text. A sequential three-day unit was developed, utilizing the book and the songs. The students were told to find as many curricular areas as possible to integrate with the book/songs during the duration of the unit. They produced visual aids, a sequential, detailed plan for each subject integration, along with creative ideas for classroom implementation. In the process of assembling the unit, the students found themselves leaping over curricular boundaries, brainstorming with friends, and, on the whole, stretching the self-imposed limits of their creativity. If their actual classrooms resemble the written product at all, they will be exciting places to learn. Sadly, the application is not always successful or seen as necessary.

The Courage to Guess
One of the most memorable aspects of my archives research was the opportunity to examine handwritten pieces of Bruner's correspondences and personal notes. Included in one of the boxes was a galley of *The*

Process of Education that had, in his handwriting, bits of marginalia. One such fragment was in the margin of chapter 4. It simply said, "The courage to guess, the courage to err."[27] This leads to the next element that should encourage intuitive responses—that of guessing.

Traditionally, guessing has received a lukewarm reception in academic circles. However, it seems to be a very natural way for an individual who is on a quest for knowledge to move closer to its discovery. My preschooler is constantly in a state of inquiry these days. The questions involve straight-forward curiosity such as, "Why is that man doing that, Mommy?" Instead of just replying to her question, we usually rephrase the query to sound like "Why do you *think* the man is doing that?" She provides her view of the situation, drawing on what she already brings to the event. We don't always respond positively, but if it is a logical guess or even a cre-ative one, we tell her so. Then we briefly confirm her guess or help her to create an accurate assessment of the scene.

Several times in the course of Bruner's writings, he extolled the virtues of guessing in the process of learning and thinking. In *The Process of Education*, he wrote that "mastery of the fundamental ideas of a field involves not only grasping of general principles, but also the development of an attitude toward learning and inquiry, toward guessing and hunches, toward the possibility of solving problems on one's own."[28] Perhaps we can liken informed guessing to musical improvisation. A beginning jazz musician knows enough of the rudiments and elements of music to read musical notation and has sufficiently mastered the ability to transfer that written notation to actual sound. Knowing the harmonic parameters of a piece of music (i.e., what chords sustain the melody line), she can then begin to musically *guess* by playing different melodic fragments that fall within the chord structure. She may choose to imitate the rhythmic mo-tives previously heard in the piece or experiment with new ones. The trial and error process of early jazz improvisation often does not offer appeal-ing listening experiences, but it is the best way for young musicians to make the connection between what they see, what they hear, and what they know.

Bruner reminds us that the "shrewd guess" and the "fertile hypoth-esis" are important tools in the thinking process. You can often solve a mystery without first uncovering all the clues. The fictional Sherlock Holmes became a master in the art of heuristics, uncovering what he could and deducing the rest, while teaching Dr. Watson to do the same for himself. According to Bruner, any teacher who says "you're only guessing" should be "tried as an educational criminal" primarily because such a statement is an attack against intellectual inquiry.[29] He advocated following up the guessing process with verification and confirmation and lamented the tendency to avoid the act of guessing altogether by asking if it is better for students to just sit mute.[30]

Our task is to help the student find a delicate speculative balance. We need to learn how to teach the student to

> . . . cut his losses but at the same time be persistent in trying out an idea; to risk forming an early hunch without at the same time formulating one *so* early and with so little evidence as to be stuck with it waiting for appropriate evidence to materialize; to pose good testable guesses that are neither too brittle nor too sinuously incorrigible.[31]

Did I Get an "A"?

Facilitating the leap between learning and thinking may be further stimulated by a re-examination of external rewards and the grading system. Bruner said that "the will to learn is an intrinsic motive, one that finds both its source and its rewards in its own exercise."[32] One would hope that juniors and seniors in college would pursue learning for the sheer love of it and for the potential betterment of humanity. However, for far too many of them, learning has become a cued response with the expected outcome being some kind of reward. How many times have I labored over my comments on a student's assignment, hoping that learning would be enhanced and dialogue begun once the comments were read, digested, and subsequently applied to a new task. Unfortunately, most times the comments are bypassed for a hurried glance at the ubiquitous grade and that ever-present "How-come-you-didn't-give-me-an-A" look (note the implied abdication of responsibility as well). The external grading system in place in most systems of higher education is just one example of an extrinsic motivator, but it is, without a doubt, the most influential one. It would be naive to suggest that the system be abandoned altogether, but perhaps a balance needs to be taken within the methods classroom. This is particularly true if we want to show preservice educators that they can break the unending reliance upon extrinsic motivators in their own future classrooms.

It is fairly obvious that when an individual approaches a task for the first time, he will rely on some sort of extrinsic motivator to sustain interest and provide some measure of increasing levels of competence. Bruner agreed that short-term behavior can be shaped by extrinsic rewards—that success followed by reward will no doubt produce similar repeat performances. If there is too little extrinsic reward, there is a danger of reduction of effort.

However, too keen a reliance upon extrinsic motivators can produce students who offer rote, predictable, stereotypic responses with little depth of learning. "The danger is creating dependence in the learner upon the reward and the rewarder to keep the behavior going. Optimum phasing requires a gradual process of giving the rewarding function back to the task and the learner."[33]

According to Bruner, curiosity and the drive to achieve competence are important cogs in the wheel of intrinsic motivation and the push for effective cognitive learning. An intrinsic motive does not depend upon reward outside of the activity in order to sustain it over the long term. The challenge, then, is to facilitate the students' move from short-term skill proficiencies (propelled mostly by extrinsic motivators) to long-range skill mastery (sustained by intrinsic satisfaction of problem solving success). How do we work under the ever-present grading system while providing opportunities for students to accomplish tasks without excessive penalties or sufficient chances to move to a higher level of learning through intrinsic motivation?

I will never forget how one graduate professor tried to move in this general direction. If we met all the requirements for the course in a satisfactory way (competence was set at 85%), then we all received a B. If we chose to try for an A, we were to do a final creative competency project. We were given no parameters except that the content of the project should reflect some aspect of the course content. Our first reaction, as grade-obsessed graduate students, was to balk at such a loosely defined, seemingly arbitrary assignment. Of course, we had the option of choosing a B by not turning in the project. Some students made murals, mobiles, and incredibly decorative visual representations of aspects of the course content while others went the more conservative analysis route. I analyzed poetry for its behavioral references and thoroughly enjoyed the assignment. In retrospect, I realize that the professor was encouraging us to examine our motivations for performing these tasks. It was a practical object lesson that worked.

He even challenged us to choose to get a B in order to experience the liberation that would accompany the act. I took him up on the challenge and chose *not* to study much for an opera literature final. That was the only B of my entire graduate career—with no regrets.

Perhaps we need to experiment with competency-based grading systems, grade contracts, conferences where students contribute self-assessment (quite literally grading their own performances), or even pass/fail strategies. Each time teacher educators encourage the leap between learning and thinking through depth of coverage, each time we stress accountability, intuition, and guessing, and each time we modify the structure of evaluative processes, we expose the learner to new connections. Perhaps subsequent hurdles won't appear as insurmountable, and they will be ready for the next level—the opportunity to *apply* what they have learned.

Notes

1. P. Castelli (personal communication, August 8, 1996).

2. D. R. Olson & J. S. Bruner. (1996). Folk psychology and folk pedagogy. In D. R. Olson & N. Torrance (Eds.), *The handbook of education and human development* (pp. 9–27). Cambridge, MA: Blackwell, 9.

3. J. S. Bruner. (1959). Learning and thinking. *Harvard Educational Review, 29*(3), 184, 187.

4. J. S. Bruner. (1973). *The relevance of education.* New York: W. W. Norton, 60.

5. J. S. Bruner. (1992). Science education and teachers: A Karplus lecture. *Journal of Science Education and Technology, 1*(1), 12.

6. J. Bruner (personal communications, February 8, 24, and May 1, 1996).

7. J. S. Bruner. (1965). The growth of mind. *American Psychologist, 20,* 51.

8. J. S. Bruner. (1980). Jerome S. Bruner. In G. Lindzey (Ed.), *A history of psychology in autobiography, Vol. 7* (pp. 75–151). San Francisco: W. H. Freeman and Company, 120.

9. J. S. Bruner. (1971). The relevance of skill or the skill of relevance. In Merle E. Meyer and F. Herbert Hite (Eds.), *The application of learning principles to classroom instruction* (The First Western Symposium on Learning, October 1969). Western Washington State University, 9.

10. J. S. Bruner, Learning and thinking, 54.

11. J. S. Bruner & B. Clinchy. (1966). Toward a disciplined intuition. In J. S. Bruner (Ed.), *Learning about learning: A conference report* (ERIC Document Reproduction Service No. ED 015 492, pp. 71–83). Washington, DC: U.S. Government Printing Office, 71.

12. See the following for additional information regarding intuitive and analytical thinking: J. S. Bruner. (1960). *The process of education.* Cambridge, MA: Harvard University Press; J. S. Bruner. (1960). On learning mathematics. *The Mathematics Teacher, 53*(8), 610–619; Bruner & Clinchy, Toward a disciplined intuition; and J. S. Bruner. (1986). *Actual minds, possible worlds.* Cambridge, MA: Harvard University Press.

13. J. S. Bruner. (1979). *On knowing: Essays for the left hand.* Cambridge, MA: Harvard University Press, 57.

14. Bruner & Clinchy, 81.

15. Bruner & Clinchy, 71–72.

16.   Bruner, *The process of education*, 27.

17.   J. S. Bruner. (1966). *Toward a theory of instruction*. Cambridge, MA: Harvard University Press, 37.

18.   Bruner & Clinchy, 76.

19.   Bruner, *Actual minds, possible worlds*, 127.

20.   Bruner, *The relevance of education*, 106.

21.   J. S. Bruner & E. Hall. (1970). Bad education—A conversation with Jerome Bruner and Elizabeth Hall. *Psychology Today, 4*(7), 57.

22.   J. S. Bruner. (1996). *The culture of education*. Cambridge, MA: Harvard University Press, 52.

23.   J. Bruner (personal communication, December 5, 1995). See also chapter 3 in *The culture of education*, p. 77.

24.   J. S. Bruner. (1963). Structures in learning. *NEA Journal, 52*(3), 26.

25.   J. S. Bruner. (1983). *In search of mind: Essays in autobiography*. New York: Harper and Row, 183.

26.   D. DeNicola. (1991). In memoriam. *Proteus: A Journal of Ideas, 8*(1), 16.

27.   Bruner Papers, HUG 4242.40, Harvard University Archives.

28.   Bruner, *The process of education*, 120.

29.   Bruner & Hall, Bad education, 54.

30.   Bruner, *The process of education*, 62.

31.   J. S. Bruner. (1961). The act of discovery. *Harvard Educational Review, 31*, 31.

32.   Bruner, *Toward a theory of instruction*, 127.

33.   J. S. Bruner. (1966). Theorems for a theory of instruction. In J. S. Bruner (Ed.), *Learning about learning: A conference report*. (ERIC Document Reproduction Service No. ED 015 492, pp. 196–210). Washington, DC: U.S. Government Printing Office, 209.

Bruner On . . .

Infant Research

Less than one month after the birth of my second child, I wrote to Bruner, detailing my exhausting routine and the demands of being a mother to two small children. He commiserated with my state of weariness, and then he reminded me of his infant research days. Those readers who prefer the more formal account of this period may consult his intellectual autobiography.[1] I prefer the conversational tone of the following e-mail narrative (and the glimpse into his wit and humor):

> I've got to tell you a story. You know, when I was doing all that work on young infants (starting at a couple of hours of age), I knew that the only way such young kids could "respond" was by sucking. So I decided I'd better find out all there was to know about infant sucking—and a lot is known. Like, for example, that they can generate a suction pressure of ca. 30 lb. per square inch and go on doing it easily in their burst-pause pattern for an hour. So we were just rigging up our famous Harvard nipple then (of which more in a moment) and I decided I'd train myself to suck at that rate and pressure, too. Gad! I nearly *died*. I just couldn't get into that ball park. So I asked some muckamuck how come, and learned that young infants managed it because of their soi-disant adipose pads—those fat little cheeks that make them so adorable, but besides make it possible for them to suck down a house. Anyway, before I was done, I had two-week olds sucking blurry pictures of a motherly young woman into focus (to prove that William James was wrong about the world of the baby being "blurry, buzzing confusion," because they desisted from sucking when it drove the picture out of focus, etc.).
>
> Anyway, that four or five years of working with very young, prelinguistic babies (we used to call them) was enormous fun. And the work *so upset* pediatricians, they could kill me! Funny lot, those old pediatricians. I think their belief in the utter mindlessness of young babies must have given them an ego-boost![2]

Notes

1. A more complete version (with names and places) can be found in his intellectual biography located in G. Lindzey (Ed.), *History of psychology in autobiography*, Vol. 7 (pp. 75–151). San Francisco: W. H. Freeman, 134.

2. J. Bruner (personal communication, March 8, 1997).

Chapter Three

Apply, Generalize, Transfer: What's in a Word

Once students make the leap between learning and thinking, the next challenge is to provide them with opportunities to flex their application muscles. The ability to connect pieces of knowledge and to apply knowledge and skills from one learned task to another new one plays a profound role in the overall processes of thinking and learning. Some circles use the term *transfer* to describe the effect that learning one task has on the learning of another. A positive transfer usually indicates that one task facilitates the learning of another and a negative transfer implies that the first interferes with learning the second.[1] Although Bruner also used the term in *The Relevance of Education*, he recently expressed to me a dislike for a word which, by his accounts, doesn't capture the essence of the connection process.

The idea of transfer has its roots in behaviorist learning theory ("transfer of response" or "transfer of identical elements") and Bruner regards it as "a mechanical expression that somehow misses what goes on when I recognize, say, that multiplication is just repeated addition. Or that a point makes a line when extended, a line makes a plane when extended, and a plane makes a solid when extended, which in turn tells how the equations for each of them are related."[2]

I must admit to being in the midst of an interesting conundrum. I am one of those rare breeds who has managed to peacefully coexist with my cognitivist/constructivist views and my behaviorist influences. Transfer was a word I bandied about quite freely to describe an individual's ability to connect or apply. Bruner challenged me to examine whether our different responses to the term were due to semantic or substantive interpretations. Taken from a purely theoretical point of view, his preference for the use of the words *application* or *generalizing* is probably more to the crux of the matter. Transfer, in its purest sense, implies a task-to-task relationship with little regard for how the human functions as the connec-tor. It focuses on tasks and causal relationships that do not change ("Task A's" relationship to "Task B" will either be positive or negative). The human element of interpretation is somehow missing. Point well taken . . . and applied.

Tupperware Containers

Most teachers, regardless of their discipline or their particular view of transfer, would probably agree with the following statement: "Anyone responsible for designing, managing, or conducting an instructional program knows the frustration experienced when participants in the program do not, cannot, or will not apply what supposedly *they were taught* [italics mine]."[3] For example, I take one week per semester to discuss the benefits of positive classroom management techniques with my methods classes. Within the context of these discussions, I often ask students to make concept transfers, that is, to apply the ideas examined in one setting to another venue. We examine teacher language behaviors, including the intent/function dynamic mentioned in chapter 2. We consider how their verbal interactions with the children actually function as opposed to how they may have been intended. This analysis, of course, eventually leads to a discussion of the dangers of using sarcasm in the classroom.

I then ask the students to take the intent/function dynamic from an academic setting to a social setting. Here is where the pace of the discussion usually slows down. Is it because the students are unaccustomed to connecting life events? Do they function in a compartmentalized world where few concepts are linked and life experiences are kept locked in separate Tupperware containers? The old adage that "everything relates to everything" appears lost on this generation of students. I am reminded of a phrase Bruner used in a letter to the editor of the *New York Review* in 1966. He spoke of "no-think thinking"—his context was different, but the meaning is applicable here. I believe our students are often no-think thinkers, unable to move gracefully from one concept to another and often unwilling to see the beauty in such movement. Teacher education courses contribute to this detachment when they encourage information acquisition through sound byte summaries. Some of the problem lies in the textbooks that are traditionally used in these classes. I have always been amused because so many of the texts relegate the contributions of learning theorists (such as Piaget and Bruner) to one or two paragraphs.

The danger inherent in such oversimplification and separation is that wonderfully complex and intricately related pieces of knowledge begin to translate only into "rote clichés that do indeed rattle around unconnected in the head."[4]

To be sure, being able to connect elements of a concept and apply those to another set of integers presupposes a slightly higher order of processing information. One of my favorite activities involves having the class make application to the field of music education from seemingly abstract psychological theories. For example, when we discuss Robert Gagné's eight-step learning hierarchy, I challenge them to find a musical task and describe it from inception to completion utilizing Gagné's order.[5] I've seen some interesting attempts—from the proper assemblage of the parts of a clarinet to the routine of a conductor prior to a performance.

I got a glimpse of just how important Bruner believes transfer is during a couple of our conversations. He related that as a fifteen-year-old in history class, he had the good fortune to have a teacher who truly excited both his imagination and his intellect by revealing the interconnectedness of events in history. While he doesn't recall specifics, he does

> . . . remember the frisson I felt when I realized that, for Pete's sake, the time of the French Revolution coincided with (or came right in the middle of) the period when all sorts of other things were breaking loose: music by Mozart, Haydn, Beethoven; things in physics like the invention of thermodynamics; the opening of the New World in the century preceding . . . funny that in my memory, it was as likely to be a piece of poetry that wedged my mind open as anything else. I can still recall my encounter with those lines from Blake, "The dog starved at the master's gate/Spells the downfall of the State". Things of that sort helped lead me to the idea of the structure of knowledge—something about there being a deep structure with things whether "deriving" from it (as in science) or being variations on it. So, as for the last, you can see why, since I was sixteen or seventeen, I have always thrilled to the variation form in music—whether the Goldberg, the LaFolia, or the blessed Art of the Fugue that Bach wrote for practicing with his daughter, Anna Magdalena.[6]

It is no wonder that Bruner continues to provide the same kind of application-rich learning environment today at the New York University School of Law where he often team-teaches a class on constitutional interpretation. The law students read major literary works along with standard cases. For example, he assigns *Billy Budd* during a time when the classroom discussion centers on the death penalty, capital crimes, and the interpretive decision making role of judges in such cases. Why a Melville novella alongside standard "black letter law" cases? Juxtaposing the novel next to familiar cases *defamiliarizes* those cases. According to Bruner, the examination of Billy Budd, Captain Vere, the Quartermaster, the drum-head court, and Vere's decision ("an angel must die") serves a necessary purpose—you can't start thinking about something again until it becomes *unfamiliar*.

He also asks them to illustrate their interpretations of the story of God, Abraham, and the potential sacrifice of his son, Isaac, using masks that they have made. The goal of this exercise is to get the law students to think of different perspectives that can be applied to classical accounts. He recounts the following:

> One group managed to bring in the question of why Sarah hadn't been consulted
> before the trip to Mt. Moriah (did it by having God make some asides about how
> come only Abraham and Isaac showed up). You see, Diane, law is about norma-
> tive issues, and our crippled language is never explicit enough about the norma-
> tive presupposition involved in cases or in life generally. So part of the job in
> teaching law is to get students to make the implicit and unstated explicit and
> stateable.[7]

Through these exercises, Bruner encourages students to weave cre-ativity and intuitive thinking into a fascinating web of connections with historical and classical accounts. How can *we* encourage our students to feel the same about the tasks we assign? How can we push them to find connections and applications?

In a piece of earlier research, Bruner seemed to suggest that the ways in which material is organized will either facilitate transfer or contribute to the presence of learning blocks. The study titled "Cognitive Processes in Learning Blocks" was multifaceted, but the principal question addressed was "what is it that makes it possible for a person to take advantage of past learning in such a way that it can be applied to new problems?" The report (found in the Harvard University Archives) was a preliminary one, and the subjects were students with specific learning problems. Even though the research was still in progress at the time of the written report, the role of cognitive organization and cognitive risk-taking as necessary compo-nents to successful learning and transfer seemed obvious.[8]

Transferability

In *The Relevance of Education*, Bruner identifies six hindrances to trans-fer. (I use the term here cautiously, knowing that his definition has evolved and is not contextually the same as behaviorists' definition of the word.) The student must first realize that there is a connection between data, that she can go beyond to new problem solving tasks using previously learned material (*attitude*). Next, the student needs to be able to fix the new material into what she already knows (*compatibility*). Third, the student needs to experience success with problem solving endeavors, spurring her on to further attempts (*activation*). She needs the opportunity to use the skills that require combining learned material with problem solving activities (*practice*). The student also must be able to explain or restate what she has just done (*self-loop*) and to be able to manage the amounts of material learned in order to problem solve (*information flow*). The absence or weakness of one or more of these components will, according to Bruner, impact overall effectiveness of the process.

How can methods instructors shore up these six areas in the classroom? I believe we first have to make a conscious choice to both personally model connective thinking and then to structure opportunities for connections within the classroom. Only then can we begin to influence those hard-to-reach domains such as attitude. Eliminating the attitude hindrance to transfer may be the most difficult of the six to achieve (and I am not sure it can ever be totally eradicated). Here methods teachers will no doubt feel like they are cheerleaders, encouraging the students to take what they know and to trust their own "implicit models" in order to self-realize that they can indeed go beyond the information given.[9]

I will never forget the rigorous training I received in one graduate class. The professor would periodically stop the lecture or class discussion to issue a *call for transfer*. We would have to immediately make an application from the material we had just encountered. These would assume either written or verbal form. When we were stumped, he would admonish us to "just start writing [talking]." The more *calls* we completed, the easier they became. After a while, many of us automatically began to connect seemingly unrelated concepts without prompting.

Allowing the student to think out loud may aid in the compatibility issue. If we question and probe in order to help the student restate what she knows, then she may begin to see how conceptual relationships are made and make mental and verbal connections. Or, as Bruner puts it, ". . . when you got the pupils to rephrase uses in their own terms and kept pushing them as to how something could be used, eventually they would find some place where it connected with a structured body of knowledge they already had."[10]

Activation relies on at least a modicum of success in the problem solving arena and on appropriate levels of reinforcement or reward for the exercise of thinking. However, we need to make sure our reinforcement efforts are appropriate to the situation, consistently provided, and genuinely given.[11] As mentioned earlier, structuring assignments where success is virtually assured might be a worthwhile place to begin. Success breeds success. Moreover, following close on the heels of activation is the need to provide students with enough opportunity to practice the skills used in problem solving and transfer. It is important to build some of these practice sessions within the confines of class time. The teacher can function as facilitator and soundingboard and can provide assurance that the students are on the right track before they are left to their own devices.

How many times have we witnessed a student going through the motions or doing a skill by rote and sheer repetition without the ability to explain or describe the causal relationships involved. In my twenty-plus years of teaching piano, I have lost track of the number of times I asked the question, "Why did you play it that way?" or "Can you explain how to replicate the tone color, [gesture, placement] of the last piece and apply it to this one?" without receiving a response. I believe that if students cannot describe the event in question back to themselves (the idea behind the self-loop), then they have not truly internalized the information and made it their own. The idea is not a new one: The Greeks believed that if you couldn't say it, you didn't know it. Bruner describes the phenomenon this way: "To understand something as a specific instance of a more general case—which is what understanding a more fundamental principle or structure means—is to have learned not only a specific thing, but also a model for understanding other things like it that one may encounter."[12]

I encourage students to make visual paradigms of complicated concepts. A visual representation of a difficult concept may be easier to achieve than a cogent verbal description. Note, for example, the many theorems cited in *Toward a Theory of Instruction* (1966). I was able to see their connection and relationship to cognition when I structured the information into visual diagrams because many of the figures resembled sentence diagrams or were a series of interlocking circles, arrows, and lines. Some scholars might label these visual representations as simplistic. However, I find them most helpful when I am trying to process and *retain* large amounts of information.

Students are often daunted by the task of creating a coherent, sequential, and creative unit of study. Using the models found in the book, *Course Design: A Guide to Curriculum Development for Teachers*, the students in my secondary methods and graduate curriculum classes develop conceptual maps that help them visualize the content, pacing, topical flow, relationships, and scope and sequence of their units prior to fleshing out the detail components. I have found the use of conceptual maps to be a great teaching tool and the students seem to appreciate the sense of control and vision that construction brings. I've provided a few mapping examples done by both individuals and collaborative learning teams at the end of this chapter (see Figures 2, 3, and 4).

Brainstorming sessions also provide students with opportunities to complete the self-loop in nonthreatening, informal settings. Allowing the students to brainstorm aloud in groups seems to jumpstart the transfer process regardless of whether they are trying to figure out responses to certain prescribed student behaviors or beginning to make across-the-curriculum connections.

Managing the information flow has, I believe, more to do with our modes and methods of presentation than a student's inability to grasp, sort through, process, and digest information. We need to do a much better job of, as Bruner says, converting learning into comprehensible and nutritious forms suitable for student consumption.[13] Chapter 4 will address ways in which we can restructure our curriculum in order to make information more accessible and digestible.

According to Bruner, something is indeed worth knowing if it provides a sense of sheer delight. It must also yield "the gift of intellectual travel beyond the information given, in the sense of containing within it the bases of generalization. The middling criterion is whether the knowledge is useful."[14] As our students grow more comfortable and skilled at generalizing, their remarkable journey of intellectual travel will only become easier and more enjoyable. As they begin to see the connection between ideas, thoughts, and concepts, they will hopefully begin to appreciate the economy transfer brings to the learning process. As Bruner stated in *The Process of Education*,

> . . . Teaching specific topics or skills without making clear their context in the broader fundamental structure of a field of knowledge is uneconomical . . . such teaching makes it exceedingly difficult for the student to generalize from what he has learned to what he will encounter later . . . learning that has fallen short of a grasp of general principles has little reward in terms of intellectual excitement . . . [and] knowledge one has acquired without sufficient structure to tie it together is knowledge that is likely to be forgotten.[15]

So the clarion call should be: *On to intellectual travel . . . on to economy of learning . . . on to ultimate connections . . . on to* (choose your own word) *application, generalization, and transfer.*

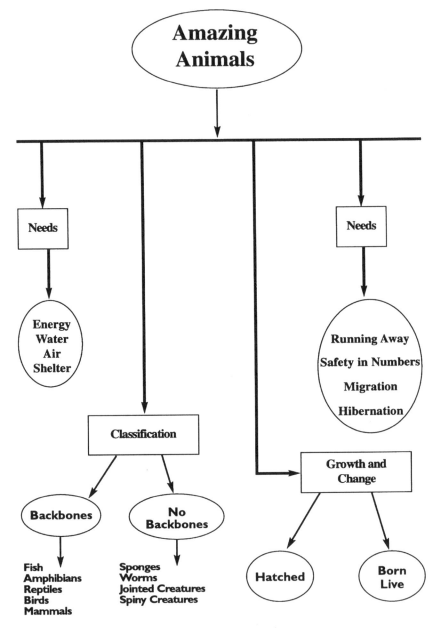

Figure 2. Example of Conceptual Map (Beverly McCall).

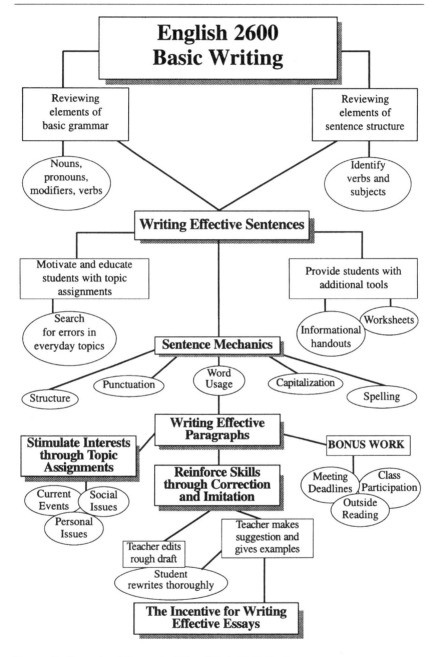

Figure 3. Example of Conceptual Map (Frieda D. Bullard).

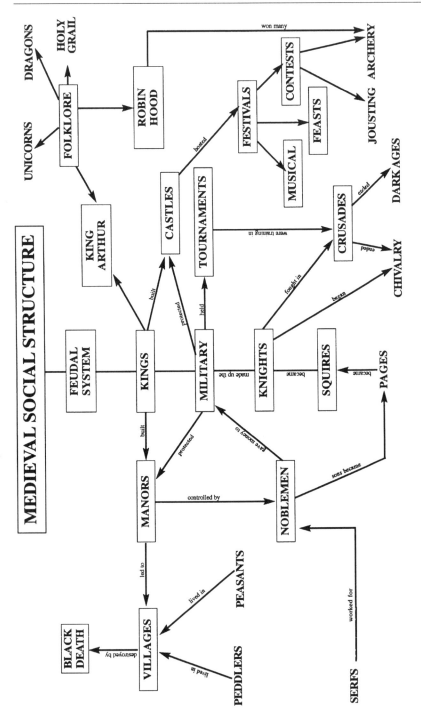

Figure 4. Example of Conceptual Map (Ward Thigpen).

Notes

1. C. H. Madsen & C. K. Madsen. (1981). *Teaching/discipline: A positive approach for educational development* (3rd ed.). Raleigh, NC: Contemporary Publishing, 278.

2. J. Bruner (personal communication, April 13, 1999).

3. L. Ehrenberg. (1983). How to ensure better transfer of learning. *Training and Development Journal, 37,* 81.

4. J. S. Bruner. (1966). Letter to the editor of the *New York Review* in response to a review of *Toward a theory of instruction* that appeared in the April 14, 1966, issue. Housed in the Harvard University Archives, HUG 4242.75.

5. R. M. Gagné. (1965). *The conditions of learning.* New York: Holt, Rinehart and Winston.

6. J. Bruner (personal communication, December 5, 1995, and April 12, 1999).

7. J. Bruner (personal communication, April 12, 1999).

8. J. S. Bruner. (1958). *Cognitive processes in learning blocks.* Harvard University, Laboratory of Social Relations. Report housed in the Harvard University Archives, HUG 4242.60. For more information, see *Bruner On . . . Learning Block Research* in this text.

9. J. S. Bruner. (1971). *The relevance of education.* New York: W.W. Norton, 71–72.

10. Bruner, *The relevance of education,* 75.

11. One of the best discussions on contingent feedback that I have found is in *Teaching/discipline: A positive approach for educational development.*

12. J. S. Bruner. (1960). *The process of education.* Cambridge, MA: Harvard University Press, 25.

13. ————, *The relevance of education,* 17.

14. ————. (1960). On learning mathematics. *The Mathematics Teacher, 53*(8), 617.

15. Bruner, *The process of education,* 31.

Bruner On . . .

Learning Block Research

Archival research is an academic's version of an archeological dig. Much of what you scrutinize is merely incidental—mostly you find a jigsaw of bits of paper, discarded airline tickets, itineraries, agendas, marginalia, and notes. It would be like an archeologist finding sand and miscellaneous detritus. But then, violá! You uncover a gem that yields much more than any investment of time or energy.

In the late 1950s, Bruner participated in research involving children with learning blocks. He never published much in this area but joined the effort both for his own enrichment as well as to help others who were involved with this research problem. I think it also may have prepared his mind and spirit for the tide of educational reform initiatives that were about to clamor for his attention.

I have selected portions of the study narrative as I found it in the Harvard University Archives. I think it has many implications toward how we instruct and assess kids with learning disabilities. Bruner recounts briefly in his intellectual autobiography that

> . . . [the study] made me very aware of the difference between coping with problem solving (what children are supposed to do in school) and defending oneself against failure-producing learning tasks inherent in school work. It gave me a very good feel, indeed, for what school looked like to children.[1]

That's a journey we all need to take together with Bruner. In order to reveal the essence of this research, I've pieced together material from the grant report that is central to the research question. There were three parts of this study, all aimed at answering one fundamental question: How does a person take advantage of past learning experiences in such a way as to be able to manage new problems that are encountered? According to Bruner, the purpose of this project was

> . . . to determine and describe the kinds of cognitive organization of learned material that facilitate and inhibit transfer of learning from one learning situation to another. Specifically, to find what kinds of "defensive organizations" operate to produce learning blocks and what kinds of "generic organizations" lead to broad transfer of learning . . . [in other words, this project focused on] modes of cognitive organization, willingness to risk with new hypotheses in problem solving, ability to handle alternatives, and methods of anticipating the consequences of success and failure.
>
> . . . we have come to learn that there is a deep and important qualitative discontinuity between the "defensive strategies" of the disturbed child with a learning block and the "coping strategies" of the child who is operating adequately in school learning. This is not to say that there is no overlap, for there patently is— notably in the *transitory anxieties of the school child who is put under undue achievement conflict,* [italics mine] when learning strategies may be replaced by defensive patterns designed to protect him from becoming involved in learning and its consequences . . . it is the difference, comparing defense and coping, between analyzing the functional paralysis of somebody who is avoiding the necessity of walking and analyzing the biodynamics of walking. One may intrude on the other, but they are in no sense on a simple continuum that permits direct comparison.
>
> . . . It is not, in the cases we have seen, that learning is of no interest to these children (often the teacher's complaint), but rather that learning is *too* consequential—almost a matter of life and death . . . learning progress becomes associated for one child with becoming independent; it also means losing a relationship of dependence on the parent. In another child, there is a deep anxiety about hostility—his own towards his parents and theirs toward him. Learning, being a counter in the strained relationship between parent and child, connotes the possibility of encountering something dangerous and hostility-evoking—either "out there" or "inside."
>
> In the first case, when the child encounters threatening material . . . the reaction is best described as "shutting down." Nothing comes to mind, the material cannot be grasped as a whole, indeed it may not even be "seen" or "heard" properly. Where the child has developed techniques for conforming to what is expected of him in school, he may handle such material by trying (often chaotically) to commit it to mind—the elements but not the overall pattern—by rote. Where the material is complex, this leads to a highly confused learning, subject not only to memory interference but to the added interferences of stress. Learning under these conditions is very slow and transfer to next tasks virtually nil.[2]

Bruner uses the term *defense by assimilation* to describe how a child with a learning challenge approaches new material. The child takes the material and codes it in terms of preemptive metaphors. These preemptive metaphors may be organized around the idea of aggression—

danger—retribution. Bruner describes the defense mechanisms that are in place when such a child approaches new material and then provides a few suggestions to neutralize the feelings of anxiety that are associated with learning.

> Virtually anything [can] arouse the defenses the child has developed for dealing with the anxiety-producing impulses involved . . . When we say "virtually anything," we do not think that this is an exaggeration. The specific case of which we speak here, for example, interprets fractions as "cut, injured numbers," cancellation as "killing off numbers on each side of the equation," [and] a graphic function as "something that will blow up any minute."
> [Tutorial therapy must include] building up confidence in the child [so] that the consequence of failure is not disaster nor the consequence of success some fantasy-inflated reward.[3]

Bruner recommends that the following elements be included in tutorial therapy:

1. child is assured that learning and consequences will not be harmful;
2. child learns to treat some learning materials/situations as neutral;
3. child will gradually risk looking at things and begin learning them; and
4. child will eventually learn to treat some areas in terms of a game with rules and procedures with meaning.

Guiding these children through cognitive risk-taking events is a pivotal step toward successful and healthy learning, and providing coping mechanisms for children seems to be paramount to successful application of learning.

> . . . inherent in the act of applying knowledge obtained in one situation to a new situation is the risk of being wrong, or making a mistake. It is our impression in the observation of classroom behavior, that the tendency to avoid errors of commission often leads to a narrowing effect—as when children will not use past arithmetic learning to solve new problems because "mistakes" are worse than "not knowing."[4]

Notes

1. J. S. Bruner. (1980). Jerome S. Bruner. In G. Lindzey (Ed.), *History of psychology in autobiography*, Vol. 7 (pp. 75–151). San Francisco: W. H. Freeman, 117.

2. J. S. Bruner. (1958). Cognitive processes in learning blocks. (United States Public Health Service Grant M-1324, housed in Harvard University Archives, HUG 4242.60). Cambridge, MA: Harvard University, Laboratory of Social Relations, Abstract, 4–7.

3. Bruner, Cognitive processes in learning blocks, 6.

4. Bruner, Cognitive processes in learning blocks, 10.

Chapter Four

Constructing the Toolshed

Bruner once told me that, as soon as you write something down on paper, you suddenly lose yourself and become defined by the words. Life and learning, he reminded me, are not static. Concepts change and evolve.[1] I couldn't help but recall this remark when I juxtaposed two Brunerian views about the nature and purpose of educational curricula:

> There is a dilemma in describing a course of study. One begins by setting forth the intellectual substance of what is to be taught. Yet if such a recounting tempts one to "get across" the subject, the ingredient of pedagogy is in jeopardy. For only in a trivial sense is a course designed to "get something across," merely to impart information. There are better means to that end than teaching. Unless the learner develops his skills, disciplines his taste, deepens his view of the world, the "something" that is got across is hardly worth the transmission.[2]
>
> Reality construction is the product of meaning making shaped by tradition and by a culture's toolkit of ways of thought. In this sense, education must be conceived as aiding young humans in learning to use the tools of meaning making and reality construction, to better adapt to the world in which they find themselves and to help in the process of changing it as required. In this sense, it can even be conceived as akin to helping people become better architects and better builders. . . . Education is not simply a technical business of well managed information processing, nor even simply a matter of applying "learning theories" to the classroom or using the results of subject-centered achievement testing. It is a complex pursuit of fitting a culture to the needs of its members and of fitting its members and their ways of knowing to the needs of the culture.[3]

A thirty-year period separates the two statements and, true to his word, we see an evolving worldview in the book, *The Culture of Education.* However, time does not significantly alter the essential meaning of his earlier message. A curriculum, which is really a miniature for the whole of education, *must* move beyond mere transmission of facts and figures. To be effective, a curriculum must change, it must move, it must perturb, and it must inform all that are involved with it—both teacher and learner.[4]

It provides the structural frame, a toolshed of sorts, within which students should be able to access all the necessary implements to build their version of the world.

Bruner has written extensively about the elements of a successful curriculum, most notably in the text *Toward a Theory of Instruction* as well as in what appears to be an outline version of the book called "Theorems for a Theory of Instruction."[5] Throughout Bruner's references to curriculum, we see areas to which he repeatedly returns. In an attempt to codify the views, let's examine what I call the three "S's" of curriculum or students, structure, and sequence. Keep in mind that there is no such thing as *the* curriculum. Bruner reminds us that

> . . . a curriculum is like an animated conversation on a topic that can never be fully defined, although one can set limits upon it. I call it an "animated" conversation not only because it is always lively if it is honest, but also because one uses animation in the broader sense–props, pictures, texts, films, and even "demonstrations." Conversation plus show-and-tell plus brooding on it all on one's own.[6]

One Size Does Not Fit All

What is really implied by the term student-centered curriculum? I believe that it primarily involves understanding and accommodating the special abilities and liabilities that any given student population brings to the learning experience. According to Bruner, any teacher approaching the task of building a curriculum or course of study must find out what problem solving skills the students have acquired. Being sensitive regarding their backgrounds (which includes personality characteristics, environment, social opportunities, and linguistic backgrounds, among others) will help the teacher determine the students' predisposition toward learning. This task would appear to be less formidable for the grade school instructor who has the good fortune to teach the same population for an entire school year than it would seem to be for secondary and postsecondary educators who greet new faces every term. However, because a curriculum needs to reflect the nature of the knower (as well as the nature of knowledge and the knowledge-getting process), it should have a certain degree of built-in flexibility.[7]

For example, although there is a prerequisite to my methods course for elementary education majors, the students' skill levels remain incredibly (and at times discouragingly) disparate. In order to begin to assess their entry level, I present them with a series of questions on the first day of class. Some of the questions deal with the theoretical subject matter of the course such as "What is 4/4 meter?" "Describe a scale in your own words," and "What does the symbol # mean?" Others are more reflective in nature and help me ascertain the students' current capacities for thoughtful discourse. The questions range from the simple ("Where do you see yourself in five years?") to the more abstract ("What is your concept of a creative classroom?"). Over the years, this exercise has provided both a thumbnail sketch of each class as well as a composite of the population throughout the years. I usually note those individuals who have a secure grasp of the subject matter and then engineer their help in dealing with others who have a weaker theoretical foundation. I can adjust the length and pace of certain learning episodes to accommodate the needs of the majority and can ascertain just how far I can push their cognitive, intuitive, and creative capacities.

Any experienced teacher will concur that due to individual differences, past learning, various stages of development, and the nature of the material (and that is just the short list), there is no magic learning formula for all—one size does not necessarily fit all.[8] Since learning is indeed "context sensitive," there is not one kind of learning nor one uniform model of the learner. It behooves us to try and provide the students with a menu of possibilities.[9] If a curriculum is to prove effective, then "it must contain different ways of activating [students], different ways of presenting sequences, different opportunities for some [students] to 'skip' parts while others work their way through, different ways of putting things. A curriculum, in short, must contain many tracks leading to the same general goal."[10]

Johann Herbart, an educational philosopher of the mid-nineteenth century, proposed a fascinating idea about the minds of students. He hypothesized that every student comes to the learning environment engrossed in his own circle of thought. The circle is made up of any thoughts, activities, or preoccupations that the student experiences prior to coming into the classroom. It is, according to Herbart, up to the instructor to be able to break through each circle of thought in order for any consequential learning to begin—a formidable task indeed.[11]

However, when it comes to structuring a course of study, perhaps we could expand the concept to include a lifetime of learning circles. Each student seems to come to us with so much educational baggage. Some of the circles of their learning experiences have proven positive, and these circles seem to link together neatly and efficiently. Others have had such negative ordeals within the various educational establishments that their learning circles often are scattered, detached, and are liabilities rather than assets in their quest for learning.

Let me offer a few examples where students have brought their complex and unique learning circles to my classroom. Michael was a talented, articulate young man who, at thirteen, was diagnosed with Tourettes' Syndrome. This neurological disorder manifested itself in different ways— Michael's body responded with physical tics, loud verbal exclamations, shouts, or yipes, and the occasional panic attack. Through medication, proper nutrition, stress reduction, and sheer willpower, Michael was able to function relatively well in the classroom. However, he lived with the stigma of this disorder on a moment-to-moment basis. During his years in school (university years included), he endured the stares, the indifference, the petulant complaints, and the downright hostility from instructors who didn't want the *inconvenience* of having Michael in their classroom. The naysayers were determined to weed him out. . . . Michael was even more determined to become a teacher.

Several of us felt it was necessary to address Michael's need for higher self-esteem and bolstered confidence level within the confines of our curricula. He did all of the assigned work along with his classmates, but he required many hours of counseling and pep talks. I fondly recall the evening Michael and I sat at my dining room table working on his résumé. When Michael's intensity level increased, so did the number and severity of his tics. So amid throaty yelps, licks on the table, jumping up and down on the floor, and the compulsion to wipe the résumé over his face from chin to hairline, we fashioned a strong vita that did justice to the professional experiences he had already accumulated. We laughed at what the neighbors might say, called the table *forever special*, and had a wonderful time as we both witnessed the scattered circles of learning finally converge for Michael. No one was happier than I to receive his call after graduation that he had been hired as a teacher or to receive the newspaper clippings reporting on his successful first few years of teaching.

Others have brought their physical, mental, and emotional challenges to the classroom including blindness, various learning disabilities, obsessive-compulsive disorders, degrees of emotional conflict, and terminal illness. Such was the case with Frieda.

More than predictably polite applause accompanied Frieda as she slowly walked across the platform to receive her undergraduate elementary education degree. At least half a dozen faculty members, who normally would be bored by the proceedings, followed her march with interest, some grinning like Chesire cats, others moved to tears. We had collectively watched Frieda battle throat cancer, enduring seemingly endless rounds of radiation, debilitating bouts of weakness, devastatingly harsh prognoses. We admired her tenacity and desire to finish the degree with dignity and integrity. We counseled, comforted, cheered, and were not hesitant to modify our curricula to accommodate her special needs. I remember one instance in which Frieda was too weak to complete a classroom teaching assignment in the local public school. I arranged for her to fulfill the requirement by videotaping the same lesson at home with her two daughters and two of their friends standing in as students. She did so and far exceeded most of the work done by her peers. The look of joy and pride on Frieda's face as she accepted her diploma was enough to soften the heart of the most seasoned academic cynic.

When I think of the term *student centered curriculum*, I still see Frieda's face. This kind of education involves understanding and accommodating the special abilities and liabilities that any given student population brings to the learning experience. I often give each of these exceptional students an informal separate assessment, not unlike an IEP (Individualized Education Plan used in special education). From this assessment, I try to adjust the course content accordingly. Truly, one size does not fit all students with exceptionalities.

There does not have to be a physical, mental, or emotional component to cause disjunct learning circles. These days, higher education is catering more to the nontraditional student. Most are older adults and carry the demands of family life in addition to their schooling. Many hold down part-time or even full-time employment and often commute some distance to attend school. They often have large time gaps in their educational backgrounds and therefore lack self-confidence in their abilities to learn like they once did. Not unlike exceptional students, their day-to-day struggle to exist and succeed in the educational system often interferes with their learning success. Once again, built-in flexibility within a course will go far in allowing these bright, mature students to gain self-confidence and to clear their pathway to success. Small accommodations often function as grand gestures for this population. For example, I expand my list of excused absences within the stated attendance policy to include "sickness of dependent children." The look of relief on the faces of my student-parents when they read this is almost embarrassing. The commuting distances can also be eased if they are allowed to complete required teaching observations and experiences in their own region rather than near the university. Although distance learning is being touted by some academics as the answer to accommodating the nontraditional student, I have my doubts as to the efficacy of these high-tech "classrooms." We will have to wait until a generation of students have completed their distance learning experience in order to assess its pedagogical strengths and shortcomings.

I believe courses can be challenging and intellectually demanding while still retaining a user-friendly approach if we remember that each student is an individual rather than merely a population or generic group. As Bruner put it,

> . . . you cannot improve the state of education without a model of the learner. Yet the model of the learner is not fixed but various. A choice of one reflects many political, practical, and cultural issues. Perhaps the best choice is not a choice of one, but an appreciation of the variety that is possible. The appreciation of that variety is what makes the practice of education something more than a scripted exercise in cultural rigidity.[12]

Curricular Superstructures

When we approach a given subject with an eye toward its study and understanding, we discover the inherent structure of the subject. As Bruner stated, "Every subject has a structure, a rightness, a beauty. It is this structure that provides the underlying simplicity of things, and it is by learning its nature that we come to appreciate the intrinsic meaning of a subject."[13]

Every legitimate subject can lay claim to an internal system of logic and order, cohesive paradigms, and various cause and effect relationships. For example, syntactical connections become clearer once a sentence is diagrammed just as the mysteries behind chemical reactions are unlocked by understanding the codependence of elements within the Periodic Table. Civics becomes more accessible by examining the process behind how a bill becomes a law just as the key structure of music can become clearer by realizing its connection to the simple whole and half step patterns in a major scale.

According to Bruner, understanding and emphasizing the structure within a subject will empower a teacher and aid the learner by improving instruction and memory, simplifying information in order to form new hypotheses, and by facilitating the organization of detailed material and transfer.

First of all, knowing and appreciating a subject's inherent structure is like assembling a puzzle. If the outside pieces are connected first, one can fit the inside pieces together more easily, following the guide of the frame. I found a handwritten note in my archival research that puts it quite plainly. Responding to the President's Panel on Education Research and Development in 1963, Bruner wrote (in some marginalia) "the more the structure, the better the instruction."[14] It is logical to assume that if the teacher thoroughly knows and understands the structure of her subject, it cannot help but aid in the quality of instruction she provides.

The next three areas involve the organization of material, memory, and simplification of information, and they are almost inseparable elements. Emphasizing structure will facilitate the organization of detailed material while at the same time increasing memory potential. Bruner stated that unless detailed material is represented in structured patterns or simplified, it will be rapidly forgotten.[15] In order for learning to be useful, we must provide students both with the how-to of knowledge acquisition as well as organizational tips on how to synthesize and carry information once it is learned. Any learner who has "flooded himself with disorganized information from unconnected hypotheses will become discouraged and confused. . . ."[16]

As I have mentioned in the previous chapter, I find it useful to distill large amounts of information into visual paradigms. If I truly understand the complexities and relationships between elements of any given body of knowledge, then I *should* be able to create a graphic representation that illustrates the dynamic structure of the subject. Some sort of diagram, flowchart or picture allows me (the learner) to structure, synthesize, and pictorially represent and store into memory material which might have been otherwise overlooked and/or forgotten.

For example, the competence model I designed (see Figure 5), based upon information in the article "The Will to Learn," shows the elements needed to achieve competence and the resulting by-products of competency. This method of representing knowledge provides me with a visual crutch, if you will, and the method serves me well during moments of retrieval or exposition. To this day, I remember the visual used to teach the order and relationships of various major and minor keys. My freshman mind loved the simplicity of design of the famous Circle of Fifths (see Figure 6). I can automatically retrieve the information contained within the circle today, but it certainly provided a needed organizational aid when I was an eighteen-year-old learner (see Figures 5 and 6 on pages 60 and 61, respectively).

Everyone should find the method of representation or simplification that works for them. Some students rely on outline form in order to structure material for easier comprehension and retention. Others read aloud into a tape player and depend upon sheer repetition for later information recovery. Whatever the method, it must organize in terms of a person's

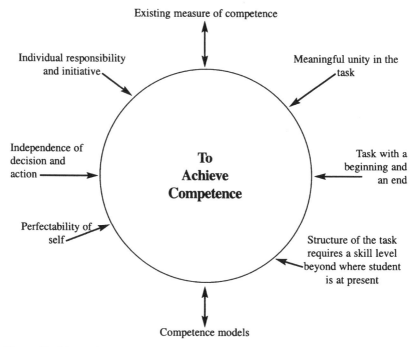

Figure 5. Major Themes in J. S. Bruner's "The Will to Learn" (*Commentary, 41*(2), 41–46).

own interests and cognitive structures in order for the information to be retrieved at a later time. In other words, it needs to be "placed along routes that are connected to one's own ways of intellectual travel."[17]

It is also helpful to provide summaries of classroom lecture material in a visual format in order to jumpstart this process for students. We should be mindful of organization in our teaching methods for "good organization achieves the kind of economical representation of facts that makes it possible to use the facts in the future . . . facts simply learned without organization are the naked and useless untruth."[18]

In a later monograph, Bruner wrote:

> Any structure of propositions . . . can, similarly, be restated in a simpler form that is both powerful and effective in the sense of being within reach of a learner. The translation may lose in power or precision, but it will still be simplifying and generative—and its gain will be in effectiveness for the user.[19]

All this talk about systematic approaches to managing the flow of information should lead us to one more important consideration. There is a danger inherent in any organizational attempt to codify material for the

Circle of Fifths

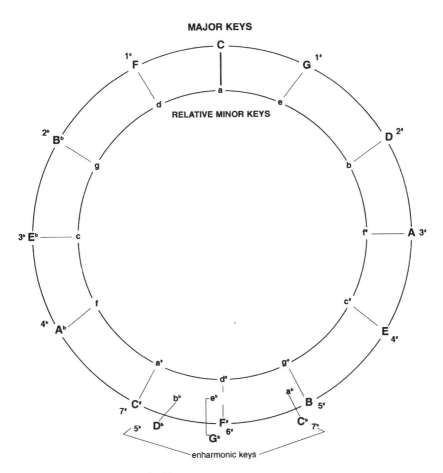

Figure 6. Musical Circle of Fifths.

learner's intellectual consumption. The danger lies in the oversimplification of material such that it loses what Bruner called its intellectual honesty. This is an issue that has remained in the forefront of my thoughts while writing this book. I'm constantly on the alert lest I commit the sin of intellectual dishonesty while attempting to synthesize or apply theoretical principles.

Even the casual Bruner reader can paraphrase the following quote from *The Relevance of Education*: "Any subject can be taught to any child at any age in some form that is both honest and powerful."[20] Those of us involved in teacher education need to be *doubly* sure that our efforts remain intellectually honest. For example, let's say I am trying to show preservice teachers how to teach the concept of high and low pitch to an early elementary population. I might assume I am being creative by making the connection between pitch and direction (high is up and low is down). However, this oversimplification doesn't ring true. Later learning will reveal that high and low can equate with right and left directionality (as in the high notes on a keyboard are to the right) or a reverse directionality (the higher strings on a guitar are at the bottom of the strum). Over the years, I have documented other inaccurate comparisons or false instructional statements (such as long = smooth; lots of notes = an interesting melody; instruments have a steady beat *in them*). Preservice educators often feel the need to water down or simplify concepts for the elementary level such that their vocabulary loses validity and has to be classified as inaccurate. Avoiding such errors will offer greater economy of learning and will eliminate multiple episodes where the same skills have to be retaught. As Bruner said, "it is as important to justify a good [Mathematics, Music, Science, English, insert your own discipline] course by the honesty it provides as by the [Mathematics, Music, Science, English . . .] it transmits."[21]

The Sequence That Binds

In order to demonstrate the relationship between structure and sequence, preservice teachers need to write task analyses. To illustrate just how they often take the steps of a given task for granted, I always begin this discussion with an object lesson. Seated before them with a bowl, spoon, and napkin, I ask the class to talk me through the steps needed to eat the bowl of oatmeal in a socially acceptable manner (i.e., the prescribed task). Because teachers rely mostly on verbal communication, I stipulate that the students cannot pantomime their directions. They must use only verbal instructions. I also inform them that I will do what they say quite literally.

The first obstacle for most students is in how to describe the act of picking up the spoon. Their verbal instructions are usually too vague and nonspecific to follow. (I see many of them trying out the movements behind their desks to see exactly *how* they perform the task.) As we proceed, they begin to see how easy it is to skip necessary steps or to micromanage the task so the steps become splintered. The students breathe a sigh of relief when the oatmeal reaches its destination and the lesson becomes apparent: It is all too easy to provide a learner with too much information, to missequence information, or to leave out significant details. The need for a step-by-step, logical, sequential approach to the dissemination of information is not only helpful, it is vital. From this point on, the task analysis becomes an organizational ally.

Just why is sequence so important? According to Bruner, there is an unbreakable bond between what is known and the order in which the knowledge is acquired. The existence of prerequisites presumes the necessity of some kind of order or sequence within any learning process.[22] Unfortunately, this area has become a sound byte for the casual Bruner reader. Far too many students of educational psychology parrot Bruner's name with the tag of "spiral curriculum" without a full understanding of its link with optimal sequencing.

The spiral curriculum is based on a system of internal prerequisites, elements of intellectual honesty (mentioned earlier), the presumption that all knowledge is connected, and the learner's involvement in the application of previously learned knowledge to future problem solving. Bruner provided this summary in his 1992 Karplus lecture:

> A long time ago, I proposed the idea of a "spiral curriculum," the idea that in teaching a subject one begins with an "intuitive" account that was well within the reach of a student and then circle back later to a more formal or highly structured account until, with however many more recyclings were necessary, the learner had mastered the topic or subject in its full generative power.[23]

It may be easy to parrot the term spiral curriculum, but it is much more difficult to create. Knowing that optimal sequences permit learners to achieve far greater leaps than they would have thought possible, I constantly feel driven to tool and retool the sequence of curricular content. It is not an overwhelming urge to create more work that drives the process, but an understanding of the nature of the learner. In *Toward a Theory of Instruction*, Bruner admonished that "there is no unique sequence for all learners, and the optimum in any particular case will depend upon a variety of factors, including past learning stage of development, nature of material and individual differences."[24] Therein lies the rub. Sensitivity to the individual differences of the learners will necessitate the development of different types of curricular sequences.

Nor can sequences be considered apart from the desired final learning outcome. According to Bruner, learning sequences include the following:

Speed of learning; resistance to forgetting; transferability of what has been learned to new instances; form of representation in terms of what has been learned in terms of cognitive strain imposed; effective power of what has been learned in terms of its generativeness of new hypotheses and combinations.[25]

It can be concluded that sequences are indeed context sensitive and subject to readiness issues. Bruner often referred to the area of mathematics for concrete examples. In discussing the importance of assessing student readiness for certain abstract concepts, he reminded us that premature use of the language of mathematics—that is, expository teaching that relies upon technical terminology, formulas, and symbolic representation—can devastate a student's confidence in her ability to do mathematics. This is because excessive formalism always portrays principles as new rather than as concepts with which the learner is already familiar. According to Bruner, if a learner has a firm grasp on, for example, the idea of comparison (one item including another or being larger than another), then she will be better disposed to understand the concept of serial ordering.[26]

The same can be said for the language of music. Music reading can be taught by using abstract, formal, and technical jargon that the learner would simply memorize and regurgitate. However, the logical, internal beauty of the musical notation system would never be appreciated, fully understood, nor used to its full potential. Students without solid backgrounds in music theory can easily be taught to parrot, "In 4/4 time, ♪ is an eighth note—it gets 1/2 beat." The words, however, are empty, meaningless, devoid of any real understanding of context. It is better to first introduce rhythmic patterns as closely resembling the rhythm of everyday speech patterns. Noteheads can be added much later to show conversion to actual notation. An illustration of this can be seen on the next page.

The fact that the students in my methods classes are more advanced in chronological age doesn't necessarily mean that they should be introduced to a concept that is new to them in an abstract way. "Readiness, I would argue, is a function not so much of maturation . . . but rather of our intention and our skill at translation of ideas into the language and concepts of the age we are teaching."[27] In many respects, my twenty-year-old preservice elementary teachers need to be initiated into music reading in the same way as would a class of kindergartners. The difference lies in the pacing. With optimal sequencing, I am able to quickly progress (in a matter of days) from prereading symbolism to actual music notation (something that may take years for young children). I love to demystify the language of music for my students. I feel that in doing so I

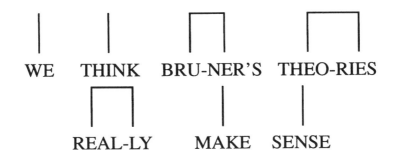

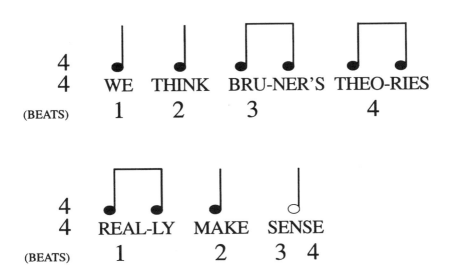

Figure 7. Turning Rhythmic Patterns into Musical Notation

am making an even greater statement about the accessibility of knowledge for the learner.

> What do we mean by an educated man? . . . an educated man should have a
> sense of what knowledge is like in some field of inquiry, to know it in its connect-
> edness and with a feeling for how the knowledge is gained. An educated man
> must not be dazzled by the myth that advanced knowledge is the result of wiz-
> ardry. I do not mean that man should be carried to the frontiers of knowledge,
> but I do mean that it is possible to take him far enough so that he himself can see
> how far he has come and by what means.[28]

Notes

1. J. Bruner (personal conversation, December 5, 1995).

2. J. S. Bruner. (1965). The growth of mind. *American Psychologist, 20,* 1911.

3. J. S. Bruner. (1996). *The culture of education.* Cambridge, MA: Harvard University Press, 20, 43.

4. J. S. Bruner. (1960). *The process of education.* Cambridge, MA: Harvard University Press, xv.

5. J. S. Bruner. (Ed.). *Learning about learning: A conference report* (ERIC Documents Reproduction Service No. ED 015 492, pp. 196–210). Washington, DC: U.S. Government Printing Office.

6. J. S. Bruner. (1992). Science education and teachers: A Karplus lecture. *Journal of Science Education and Technology, 1*(1), 5.

7. J. S. Bruner. (1966). *Toward a theory of instruction.* Cambridge, MA: Harvard University Press, 39–41.

8. Bruner, *Toward a theory of instruction,* 49.

9. J. S. Bruner. (1985). Models of the learner. *Educational Researcher, 14*(6), 5–8.

10. Bruner, *Toward a theory of instruction,* 171.

11. For additional information, please consult the following: J. F. Herbart. (1904). *Outlines of educational doctrine* (A. F. Lange, Trans.). New York: Macmillan. (Original work completed ca. 1833–1841; first known publication, 1901); J. F. Herbart. (1977). The science of education (H. Felkin & E. Felkin, Trans.). In D. D. Robinson (Ed.), *Significant contributions to the history of psychology: 1750–1920* (pp. 57–268). Washington, DC: University Publications of America. (Original work published in 1806); D. N. DeNicola. (1986). *The application of three historical perspectives on instructional language to the assessment of language behaviors of pre-service elementary and music education majors.* Unpublished doctoral dissertation, Florida State University, Tallahassee; D. N. DeNicola. (1990). Historical perspectives on instructional language as applied to an assessment of preservice teachers. *Journal of Research in Music Education, 38*(1), 49–60.

12. Bruner, Models of the learner, 8.

13. J. S. Bruner. (1963). Structures in learning. *NEA Journal,* 52(3), 26.

14. J. S. Bruner. (1963). Handwritten notes in connection with a learning project and the President's Panel on Education Research and Development. Harvard University Archives, HUG 4242.41 (box 2).

15. Bruner, *The process of education,* 24.

16. J. S. Bruner. (1961). The act of discovery. *Harvard Educational Review, 31,* 25.

17. Bruner, The act of discovery, 32.

18. J. S. Bruner. (1959). Learning and thinking. *Harvard Educational Review, 29,* 185.

19. Bruner, *Learning about learning,* 201–202.

20. J. S. Bruner. (1973). *The relevance of education.* New York: W.W. Norton, 122.

21. Bruner, *The relevance of education,* 157.

22. Bruner, *Learning about learning,* 202–203.

23. Bruner, Science education and teachers: A Karplus lecture, 7.

24. Bruner, *Toward a theory of instruction,* 49.

25. Bruner, *Toward a theory of instruction,* 50.

26. J. S. Bruner. (1960). On learning mathematics. *The Mathematics Teacher, 53*(8), 614–616.

27. Bruner, *On learning mathematics,* 616.

28. Bruner, *On learning mathematics,* 618.

Bruner On . . .

Emotional Intelligence

Bruner is a generous teacher. By that I mean that he allows for a certain degree of naiveté that is often present during inquiry. He regards thoughtful questions as legitimate and provides equally thoughtful responses.

Case in point. When I was involved in teaching a graduate curriculum class, I was introduced to the notion of emotional intelligence. While I was very familiar with Howard Gardner's idea of multiple intelligences, I really had never given much thought to the emotional intelligence domains as outlined by Peter Salovey.[1] My honest reaction was that emotional intelligence smacked of pop psychology. I failed to see why some educators would posture that ignoring the emotional "mind" ultimately would be more harmful to an individual than failing to challenge their cognitive development.

So I asked Bruner to put his spin on emotional intelligence for me. His response was characteristically informative, honest, and witty:

> Emotional intelligence is surely an absurd idea. If there is such a "thing," it consists of learning to stay out of situations that you can't manage when you're emotionally aroused, or letting people know what's exciting you off track—both of which involve, first, knowing your own feelings (intrapersonal intelligence), and second, how others are construing how you are reacting (which is interpersonal intelligence). The reason I say this is that I don't think "emotion" is cognitive or is mediated by reflection—a view best argued by Bob Zajonc. More typically, you get a "surge" of emotion, then put your mind to justifying why you feel you just LOVE Luisa like mad, DISTRUST Helena as a snake, would MURDER anyone who did any harm to David, etc. Those are usually little narratives about "why" I love Luisa, hate Helena, defend David.[2]

Notes

1. See H. Gardner. (1985). *Frames of mind.* New York: Basic Books; D. Goleman. (1995). *Emotional intelligence.* New York: Bantam Books.

2. J. Bruner (personal communication, January 25, 1998).

Chapter Five

The Buck Stops Here

By virtue of our subject matter, teacher educators *should* be among the finest teachers in the world. After all, if we are teaching others the key elements necessary for successful teaching, then it follows that we should be ideal pedagogical models. Even so, there are countless examples of theory to practice gaps in teacher education classes. We can begin to bridge the gaps by focusing on the needs of the learner, for Bruner reminds us that "growth of mind is always growth assisted from the outside."[1] We also need to understand that to be a pedagogical model requires a cutting edge and mentor mentality in addition to a strong, competent, and inspiring classroom presence.

There is no Brunerian teacher's creed, but if there was one, perhaps it would sound something like this:

Let me be a day-to-day working model of what it means to be a teacher. Let me do this, not so you will emulate the model, but so you will find my words credible and my actions resonant. Then perhaps you will let me become part of your internal dialogue. We can go on to build a relationship of mutual respect and trust, and, just maybe, you will want to make my standards your own. [2]

Aiding and Abetting

Getting to know something is an adventure in how to account for a great many things that you encounter in as simple and elegant a way as possible. And there are lots of ways of getting to that point, lots of different ways. And you don't really ever get there unless you do it, as a learner, on your own terms . . . All you can do for a learner enroute to their forming a view of their own is to aid and abet them on their own voyage.[3]

Bruner has spent a lifetime musing about how human beings learn and how perceptions of the learning process shape instructional techniques.

The learning/thinking/instructing paradigm is understandably multifaceted and complex. Perhaps it is the inherent complexity within the learning dynamic that tempts us to minimize its importance, particularly in the education of young adult minds. It is always difficult to apply theory to practice and Bruner admitted that the application of the psychological principles of learning to educational settings is no exception.[4]

However, I believe it is essential in any discussion of the attributes of teacher education, to *first* apply the magnifying glass to the learners who sit in our classrooms. Granted, our view will be generalized because there is not one kind of learning nor a single fixed model of the learner. However, Bruner reminds us that

> You do not quite need a different model of a learner to talk about learning how to play chess, learning how to play the flute, linguistics, and learning how to read the sprung rhymes in the verse of Gerard Manley Hopkins . . . learning is indeed context sensitive, but that human beings, given their peculiarly human competence, are capable of adapting their approach to the demands of different contexts.[5]

Chapter 2 of *The Culture of Education* provides a comprehensive examination of four models of the learner with the idea that "once we recognize that a teacher's conception of a learner shapes the instruction he or she employs, then equipping teachers (or parents) with the best available theory of the child's mind becomes crucial. . . ." [6] Allow me to provide a synopsis of the four learning models and the pedagogical practices that may result from each way of thinking. For the sake of example, I'll provide applications to the discipline of music.

Model One is by far the simplest to describe. Bruner calls this dynamic the acquisition of "know how." It provides us with the most basic connection between teacher and learner—the "do as I do" or rote learning process. The teacher, as role model, instructs primarily by demonstration, and the student learns mainly by imitation. This learning environment is an apprenticeship of sorts where the student attempts to become competent through practice (under the watchful eye of the teacher).

For example, the tradition of vocal music was historically transmitted through a call-and-response technique. Depending upon the setting, the leader (field steward or clergy) would sing a phrase and the group (fieldhands or church congregation) would echo the phrase in response. This imitative learning style (or rote technique) is basic and useful in skill transmission, assimilation, and production. However, we need to remember that while learning to perform skillfully is noteworthy, it does not ". . . get one to the same level of flexible skill as when one learns by a combination of practice and conceptual explanation."[7]

After I shared this application of Model One with Bruner, he chided me for being so directly pedagogical! He is right—there are myriads of subtle layers at work in all of the models, for human interaction is never predictable and rarely is it definitive. Model One can be operational even when the mentor doesn't *intend* to mentor or when the result is deliberately antithetical to the performance norm. Bruner illustrated with the following:

> I heard a brilliant string quintet rendering of *Eine Kleine Nachtmusik* at Alice Tully the other evening and it was played almost explicitly to differentiate it from the schmaltzy version you usually hear from string orchestras. Surely the "do as I do" model goes beyond just sheer imitating. The history of music surely tells us that. That must even be true of kids with their music teachers! I even have the sense that Johann Sebastian was doing what he did in Art of the Fugue to make little Anna Magdalena aware that "imitation" (as in the idea of imitation) can be a first step toward variation.[8]

Model Two is representative of the acquisition of propositional knowledge with objective tests being the assessment tool of choice for institutional analysts that crave a bottom-line measure of this learning model. From what I can gather, here the teacher conducts a predominantly one-way conversation in order to provide facts, principles, and rules from a variety of sources (including their own knowledge base, books, articles, databases, and so forth). With the a priori understanding that students bring certain mental abilities to the task, they become passive receptors for the transmitted knowledge. They may listen, take notes, and look up sources, but interplay between teacher and students is minimal.

To continue with the vocal music analogy, in this model the teacher would provide certain facts about a song, including the theory behind proper singing techniques. No music would be heard, but the students would be evaluated on their book knowledge, usually by some pencil/paper method.[9] This model is, by far, my least favorite. Unfortunately, because it requires a minute amount of creative thought and energy on behalf of teacher *and* student, we tend to see it represented far too often in classrooms of all levels and disciplines. I find it rather dismaying that so many education classes seem to have almost exclusively resorted to this form of information dissemination.

Model Three approaches the learner as thinker and views the learning dynamic as a perpetual exchange of ideas. This paradigm is not one-sided and relies heavily upon reaching a meeting of the minds through individual reflection and group discussion, collaboration, and negotiation. Each individual involved in this model reflects within themselves, shares their reflections with the group, and enters into a learning partnership with the teacher and the other students.

This model seems to be much less patronizing toward the learner's mind and what he or she already brings to the task. Bruner discussed the impact of recent research on this model, including intersubjectivity (reading other minds), theories of mind (how learners acquire their views of how others come to hold or give up certain mental states), metacognition (thinking about learning, remembering, and thinking), and collaborative learning (how learners explain and revise their positions in discourse).[10] One possible application would find the teacher working with several learners, asking them to listen and critique their peers' musical performances as well as their own. The resulting environment has the potential to come alive with the exchange of ideas, rationales, deliberations, and even negotiations.

I tell my young pianists that they cannot operate in a vacuum. They have to nurture a repertoire of musical responses—to go into that warehouse in order to make informed, sensitive, historically accurate, and musically sound performance decisions. For example, in the warehouse, we find how other performers have interpreted the pieces that they are studying. Playing three different versions of the opening motif (also repeated three times) in Beethoven's *Pathetique* Piano Sonata can provide glimpses into stylistic variations, dynamic contrasts, phrasing subtleties, shading, tempo, and intensity variations, to name a few. Here, the teacher can and should include her own interpretation among the recorded examples. Having an instructor as a performance model goes a long way toward building student-teacher respect and critical listening and evaluative skills. Of course, there is nothing like being caught up in the drama of a live performance, which even the highest quality compact disc can't duplicate. I remember one recital given by André Michel Schub that left me speechless. As an instructor, I long for my students to have a warehouse *full* of such events. I guarantee they will never play (or teach) the same again.[11]

Bruner recalled a similar foray:

> I remember I had two recordings of Schubert songs, one by Elizabeth Schwartzkopf and the other by Hilde Gueden—both remarkable, each incommensurate with the other. I must confess I've been in love all my life with Schwartzkopf, ever since hearing/seeing her do the Contessa Almaviva in *Nozze de Figaro*. So I, of course, had her version as my prototype—and I know I'm a sucker for prototypes. But I didn't "understand" Schwartzkopf's Schubert until I heard Gueden. So now the two of them entered my "community" of performances. And I couldn't wait to

play the two recordings for a friend of mine who also cherished Schubert lieder. So the community idea has a very wide applicability, I think.[12]

In Model Four, the learner is knowledgeable but must be shown how to manage objective personal knowledge with the cultural knowledge pool while understanding the interconnectedness of both with the history of knowledge.[13] Model Four capitalizes on the students' a priori knowledge of the subject, and prior experiences are factored into the teaching/learning dynamic. In other words, the student comes to the table with a personal knowledge of their culture or what has gone into making them who they are. This includes the accumulation of experiences, events, personal narratives, and the three "T's"—traumas, triumphs, and tragedies. The teacher's job is to find opportunities to enable the student to apply and connect their versions of the world with the subject at hand.

To extend our music analogy one step further, the teacher would help the students to connect these life experiences to the interpretation, expression, and performance of the song. I often joke with my very young freshmen piano majors that until they have had their hearts broken a time or two or have experienced deep passion or intense sorrow, they will truly never be able to access the requisite emotions (the Sturm und Drang) of many of the composers of the Romantic Period. "Go and live," I tell them. Then you'll comprehend and be able to move beyond technical proficiency to artistic interpretation and emotional transcendency.

Models Three and Four are ideal for studio master classes. My piano majors come every two weeks to studio class. We sit around the piano studio, and all assume the roles of audience, critic, and pedagogue. I recall one afternoon where a young (freshman) woman was playing a tricky variation which involved a lot of octave work. She turned toward the group and asked for suggestions. Should it be pedalled? How much finger connection? If I do it this way, my wrist hurts. Soon her fellow pianists were all hopping up to try the passage, giving suggestions, admonishing against stress injury. I sat as observer. Finally, they turned to me, and I only had to assume the role of clean-up batter with one personal anecdote describing how I had too much tension playing the octaves in Liszt's *Eleventh Hungarian Rhapsody* and wound up in a sling for two months. After the interchange, the synapses were firing among this band of learners, and it underscored the vital nature of the learning dynamics inherent in the last two models.

While considering the impact of these learning models, we must remember one very basic but pivotal tenet:

Real schooling, of course, is never confined to one model of the learner or one model of teaching . . . any choice of pedagogical practice implies a conception of the learner and may, in time, be adopted by him or her as the appropriate way of thinking about the learning process. For a choice of pedagogy inevitably communicates a conception of the learning process and the learner. Pedagogy is never innocent. It is a medium that carries its own message.[14]

All four visual models of the learner demonstrate that the learning process is an organic, reciprocal exchange and does not take place in a vacuum. Nor is it the same from learning episode to episode. Bruner admonished that "different approaches to learning and different forms of instruction—from imitation, to instruction, to discovery, to collaboration—reflect differing beliefs and assumptions about the learner—from actor, to knower, to private experiences, to collaborative thinker."[15] My own teaching style relies heavily on the learning dynamics as outlined in Models One, Three, and Four and is subject to modification based upon the learner and the subject matter. Much of what I do in the methods classroom lends itself to the collaborative nature of the third model while my applied music instruction (i.e., piano lessons) fits well into Model One, particularly when the subject is a beginner. Regardless, once we understand the dynamics of learning, our teaching techniques should contribute to the learning dialogue. According to Bruner, our pedagogical goals should foster independent thinking, encourage discovery, and instill confidence in an environment that favors play and conjecture.

The Discovery Zone

I encourage my seven-year-old to think independently and yet when she does (and it doesn't coincide with *my* way of thinking), it leaves me somewhat unsettled and uneasy. I think the same is true in the classroom. In theory, most teachers would probably admit to wanting their students to make decisions in the learning process that are separate from their own. However, when the result of such autonomy strays from the prescribed script, teachers are often at a loss for appropriate responses.

One of the reasons for our uneasiness regarding the issue of independent thinking may result in perceptions of what a teacher should be doing in the classroom. The second learning model describes the stereotypical arrangement of teacher as the center of all knowledge (or the "I-am-the-great-and-powerful-Oz-hear-me" syndrome). The instructor imparts knowledge to the learner who functions as an information receptor that ultimately regurgitates that material (often in scantron bubbles). This arrangement, while appropriate in some educational settings, should not be the instructional method of choice for teacher education programs.

Throughout his career, Bruner has been a champion for independent reasoning and has offered suggestions as to how we might support the process. The following synthesizes some of his recurrent variations on this theme:

1. Instructor should pull back from between the learner and the materials.
2. Instead of just processing the known, instruct the learner on how to approach the unknown by teaching the art of questioning.
3. Give students a firm grasp of the subject and make them autonomous and self-propelled thinkers.
4. Allow learners to do as much as possible for themselves and save direct intervention for later.
5. Put together exercises or experiences that lead the students to find the next step rather than merely providing irrelevant material that the student must first wade through.

In "The Act of Discovery," Bruner gives an example of several groups of children who were assigned word pairs. One group was told to remember the pairs simply by remembering. The second set was admonished to use assigned associations as mnemonic devices, and the third group was asked to create their own word associations. Not surprisingly, the students who designed their own word associations retained the second word up to 95% of the time while the other two, less than 50%.[16]

I love the phrase "Discovery, like surprise, favors the well-prepared mind."[17] I think we have to push past the notion that a classroom environment that encourages discovery and independent thought (and these are dependent variables) has to resemble a free-for-all. Discovery is not serendipitously finding a pot of gold at the end of the rainbow but the process of mining for that gold. The *process* of discovery encourages the attitude of working. In other words, "Discovery, with the understanding and mastery it implies, becomes its own reward, a reward that is intrinsic to the activity of working. . . . If emphasis upon discovery has the effect of producing a more active approach to learning and thinking, the technical problems are worth the trouble."[18]

When we lead our students toward discovery and autonomy in the learning process, we are actually allowing them to make better sense of their own world. I could ramble on about the virtues of teaching across the curriculum, but until students ferret out ideas to construct their own interdisciplinary unit, integration remains a nice theory. For example, when I assign elementary methods classes the task of creating a three-day unit that pulls in as many subject areas as possible, the jumping-off point is often an age-appropriate book that has some connection to music. One student, writing for a kindergarten population, chose the book *Berlioz the Bear*. The focus of her unit was the letter "B," but look at how many creative paths took her toward this goal. Through this activity, the student became a constructionist. The following list was from Day One of her unit[19]:

- Write the letter "B"
- Create a word wall with words that begin with "B"
- Read about bees and their habitat (found in book)
- Teach song *I'm Bringing Home a Baby Bumblebee*
- Allow children to creatively move scarfs to *The Flight of the Bumblebee*
- Plant bean sprouts using sponge in baby food jar and estimate the number of beans in a container
- Write a cinquain about bees and decorate with thumbprints
- Create a butterfly blotto
- Make and eat bugs-on-a-branch (celery stalks, peanut butter, and raisins)
- Teach the fingerplay *Here Is the Beehive*

So to exile discovery learning because of a misunderstanding of function and outcome is unfortunate:

> Discovery, whether by a schoolboy going it on his own or by a scientist, is most often a matter of rearranging or transforming evidence in such a way that one is now enabled to go beyond the evidence to new insights. Discovery involves the finding of the right structure, the meaningfulness.[20]

But What If?

What if we were to think of discovery learning as a hothouse tomato? The vine will thrive if the greenhouse has suitable temperature, humidity, soil moisture, and light. Classrooms are like greenhouses in that they can cultivate learning vines by incorporating the elements of conjecture and play into the daily routine. I love the little anecdote about the boy and the baboon in Bruner's article "The Growth of Mind." He related that a fifth-grade class was having a discussion about the organization within a baboon troop. One of the students posed a question that was theoretically impossible. Bruner subsequently relates what happened:

> [The] question could have been answered empirically—and the inquiry ended . . .
> fortunately it was not. For the question opens up the deep issues of what might
> be and why it is not. . . . It is such conjecture that produces rational, self-
> conscious problem-finding behavior so crucial to the growth of intellectual power.
> Given the materials, given some background and encouragement, teachers like it
> as much as the students.[21]

I can hear the critics now. "Oh, sure. In theory, adding the element of conjecture into the daily classroom mix sounds great. But where do you get the guidance for such an approach? If the typical teacher educator can't find it in an outline, a book, or a study guide, then he probably won't attempt it—particularly if he feels uncomfortable in this kind of specula-tive environment. For crying out loud, it's like walking a tightrope without a net!"

Precisely. Someone somewhere had to stew, muse, debate, or hypoth-esize in order to, as Bruner said, bring a body of knowledge into being, give it life and direction and sustain its growth. He further charged that the task of curriculum maker and teacher is to make sure that the students are given occasions for the exercise and nurturing of a sense of conjecture and dilemma.[22] I guarantee that if we swing open the windows to let a little conjecture and dilemma in our classrooms, the air currents would invigorate both student and teacher.

But what about the element of fun? When I was trying to ferret out the the major points in *Toward a Theory of Instruction*, I created a diagram for myself that illustrated Bruner's suggestions regarding which elements were necessary for effective cognitive learning. I found that *play* was on an equal footing with sequencing, competence, freedom from anxiety and drive, reinforcement issues, exploration of alternatives, nurturing, and intrinsic motivation. I always marvel at classrooms that are devoid of laughter, whimsy, and gentle humor. Any teacher who understands the learner and the process of learning knows that any task needs to be enter-taining, challenging, multifaceted, interesting, and fun. Bruner noted that it should be "feature rich" and one that continuously yields knowledge.[23]

Now we know that, as Bruner stated, play is the business of childhood. However, I believe that we can make the application to any learner. He reported that, after having studied hundreds of hours of play behavior, he had never seen "a child glaze over or drop out or otherwise turn off while engaged in play." He also stated that "I wish I could say the same for the children I have observed in classrooms and even in one-to-one tutorials. This leads me to wonder whether play is not quite different from work, by which I mean the classical model of problem solving with the goal held constant and the means varied."[24] In the *Ethos* article, Bruner once again reiterated the symbiotic relationship between play and work and the interconnectedness between thought, concept formation, work, and play.[25] I'm a perfect example of this play-work concept. I'm energized by the work of writing and researching, although I rarely view the process as laborious. I'm having fun—what better way could there be to view the life of the mind and its tangible results? I wish we could convince our students of the same.

That's the true spirit of the work-play concept. However, on a more basic, pragmatic level, college students are no different in this regard from their younger counterparts. Never underestimate the power of a funny anecdote or dramatic gesture to bring the class back around if they are "drifting away." You know the look—the glazed and drooping eyes, the slumped shoulders, the automatic, seemingly robotic nod of the head that is supposed to make them look on-task (but is really a mask for fatigue and boredom). In this respect, every teacher should have a touch of the actor/entertainer within and should be willing to use it to engage the learner. My husband teaches World Literature for the general studies component—a classic environment for the reluctant learner. He relates that in Book Five of *The Odyssey*, Odysseus washes up on shore, more dead than alive. In order to further understand the passage, he lays himself over the desk as he recites the text: "His knees buckled, his arms gave way beneath him, all vital force now conquered by the sea. Swollen from head to foot he was, and seawater gushed from his mouth and nostrils. There he lay, scarce drawing breath, unstirring, deathly spent." My husband lifts his head and says, "Now picture me naked." This, of course, elicits a collective chuckle from the classroom. He is now positioned, and the students' attention is riveted. They will, no doubt, attend to Odysseus' words "What more can this hulk suffer? What comes now? . . ." as my husband utters them from his position on the desk more than they would have if he remained behind the podium, aloof and detached from the text.[26] We desperately need to make school a place where the "head and the heart are fully engaged."[27] Humor can be one of our allies in this quest.

Finally, teacher educators should focus on the confidence level of our students. They need to have, according to Bruner, ". . . some degree of self-confidence before [they] can start on a task, the act of starting itself increases one's confidence in the ability to carry the task through. Gifted teachers often report that their first task is to give students the notion that their minds can be used as instruments."[28]

I always inform the students that my view of them may be different from other instructors. I do not view them as *trainees who would be teachers* but as *teachers-in-training*. I take the opportunity to remind them that the job fairy will not sprinkle magic dust on them the moment they sign their first teaching contract. They must view themselves as having the general propensities and characteristics of teachers *already* and that they are in school to continue to build upon their knowledge base, nurture their intuitive capacities, and refine their communication and presentation skills. It is amazing to see how a small paradigmal shift in thought can have a positive effect upon their attitude (more professional), their aptitude (they tend to work harder to reach a higher standard), and their levels of self-confidence and competence. If, as Bruner said, school is hard on a child's self-esteem, I often wonder whether postsecondary experiences extend the abuse. By the time students reach their early twenties, one would assume that their self-confidence would not need continual boosts from me. However, I find that old wounds often lie close to the surface, and students who have struggled with esteem issues still do fight the demons. Therefore, I believe that we can apply Bruner's suggestion to their population as well:

> The management of self-esteem is never simple and never settled, and its state is affected powerfully by the availability of supports provided from the outside. These supports are hardly mysterious or exotic. They include such homely resorts as a second chance, honor for a good if unsuccessful try, but above all the chance for discourse that permits one to find out why or how things didn't work out as planned.[29]

It seems like the least we can do.

Do as I Do and Say

Do most methods instructors view themselves as *on-the-job heroes*? Bruner, in "The Will to Learn," stresses the need to provide all learners with competence models. These individuals would not place themselves on a pedestal to be imitated but would actually become part of the students' internal dialogues.[30]

I have always been convinced that anyone who claims to be a teacher educator should be held to a higher pedagogical standard than the rest. After all, our daily focus is on the process of teaching and learning and method instructors who do not hold themselves to the highest personal standards can be justifiably branded as hypocrites. We should be able to say to our preteachers: "You can trust that what I am telling you is the most current and accurate information that is available and that I will continue to try and engage you in the learning process through a variety of pedagogical means. I will do so in an intellectually honest and stimulating fashion—one that will hopefully captivate your imagination and provoke inquiry. It is my desire that you will, in turn, teach others in similar fashion."

The first part of this pedagogical creed deals with the instructor's approach to subject matter. I'm not sure how teachers' words can have resonance and validity if they do not have a firm grasp of their respective subject. Bruner compared learning to be skillful with a body of knowledge to the intricacies and nuances of learning a language.[31] The process includes, among other things, the mastery of rules, vocabulary, semantic markers, colloquial twists and turns, and idiomatic expressions. This level of learning doesn't end with a terminal graduate degree, but it must be a lifelong pursuit. Bruner reminds us that "being a teacher makes one a better learner."[32] I believe it is vital that, as teacher educators, we demonstrate this zest for learning for our students. Doing so places us in a position to make a commitment to remain on the cutting edge of emergent bodies of knowledge, to dedicate ourselves to contribute to the knowledge base within a given discipline, and to become explorers, if you will, for ways in which to bridge the theory to practice gap.

However, I think teacher educators need to go one step beyond competence in these areas. I think we need to inject a large and sincere dose of enthusiasm into our efforts. In *The Process of Education*, Bruner recorded that "the teacher is not only a communicator but a model. Somebody who does not see anything beautiful about [*insert your discipline here*] is not likely to ignite others with a sense of the intrinsic excitement of the subject."[33] I love the anecdote about Miss Orcutt that Bruner used in *Actual Minds, Possible Worlds*. Bruner was about ten and Miss Orcutt engaged him beyond mere scientific facts.

> In effect, she was inviting me to extend *my* world of wonder to encompass *hers*. She was not just *informing* me. She was, rather, negotiating the world of wonder and possibility. Molecules, solids, liquids, movements were not facts; they were to be used in pondering and imagining. Miss Orcutt was the rarity. She was a human being, not a transmission device.[34]

It is obvious from Bruner's remarks that Miss Orcutt was fascinated, not only by science, but by the wonders of human beings and their capacity to participate in the dance of reflection, of speculation, and of application. It is that precious give-and-take with students that has the potential to raise instruction to greater intellectual heights. As a result, we need to develop our empathy for students in their struggles with the learning process. Bruner recalled the example of Bob Karplus (a key figure in the curriculum reform movement of the 1960s and 1970s):

> He knew what it felt like "not to know," what it was like to be a "beginner." As a matter of temperament and principle, he knew that not knowing was the chronic condition not only of a student but also of a real scientist. That is what made him a true teacher, a truly courteous teacher.[35]

Any learning exchange between student and teacher should make both wiser and stronger. I wonder if Miss Orcutt believed in "going meta" as much as Bruner does. In many of my personal correspondences with him, he constantly reminds me to "go meta" with a problem or position or dilemma. Getting outside of the situation long enough to think about how I think about it . . . a great exercise for the mind, but a better one for the soul, and an imperative for any teacher who is striving to be a competence model

> . . . it is crucial for the pedagogical theorist and teacher alike to help [the student] to become more metacognitive—to be as aware of how she goes about her learning and thinking as she is about the subject matter she is studying. Achieving skill and accumulating knowledge are not enough. The learner can be helped to achieve full mastery by reflecting as well upon how she is going about her job and how her approach can be improved. Equipping her with a good theory of mind—or a theory of mental functioning—is one part of helping her do so.[36]

One of the most provocative statements Bruner has made about teachers is that we are, in fact, vicars of the culture. When we begin to see ourselves as a substitute voice for or an active representative of the culture, teaching takes on a whole new dimension. It transforms past subject, past curriculum, past evaluative tools to an almost *in utero* dynamic. There is something mystical about the learning process—I wish all of us would revisit what we do in these terms.

> No educational reform can get off the ground without an adult actively and honestly participating—a teacher willing and prepared to give and share aid, to comfort and to scaffold. Learning in its full complexity involves the creation and negotiation of meaning in a larger culture and the teacher is the vicar of the culture at large.[37]

Engage the Troops

I like to listen to my students' preclass informal conversations. Sometimes, I'll show up early, under the guise of setting up audiovisual equipment or to ready the room, just to seize the opportunity to eavesdrop on their concerns, their interests, their perceptions. Invariably, some of the discussion is complaint centered, and over the years I've noticed their dissatisfaction with the way they are taught. You'll hear comments like, "I think Dr. Jones knows her subject, but all she does is read aloud from the text. . . . I could do that without having to come to class!" Or "Dr. Smith tells us to present material in exciting ways . . . wish he'd practice what he preaches." This leads to the second part of the teaching dynamic involving presentation or the ability to engage the learner through a variety of pedagogical means. In one of Bruner's earlier articles, "The Act of Discovery" (1961), he offered a clear distinction between two types of pedagogical styles—namely, teaching that takes place in the expository mode and teaching that utilizes the hypothetical mode:

> In the former, the decisions concerning the mode and pace and style of exposition are principally determined by the teacher as expositor; the student is the listener. If I can put the matter in terms of structural linguistics, the speaker has a quite different set of decisions to make than the listener: The former has a wide choice of alternatives for structuring, he is anticipating paragraph content while the listener is still intent on the words, he is manipulating the content of the material by various transformations, while the listener is quite unaware of these internal manipulations. In the hypothetical mode, the teacher and the student are in a more cooperative position with respect to what in linguistics would be called "speaker's decisions." The student is not a bench-bound listener, but is taking a part in the formulation and at times may play the principal role in it. He will be aware of alternatives and may even have an "as if" attitude toward these and, as he receives information, he may evaluate it as it comes.[38]

While I think everyone would agree that expository delivery is necessary, I believe that it is imperative for teacher educators to make liberal use of the hypothetical mode. Teaching is not a pretentiously delivered monologue. One has only to be a casual observer of the cultural-psychological approach to education to see the benefits of treating the classroom as a subcommunity. The teacher assumes the role of facilitator of events, conversations, and shared experiences with all parties involved in a mutual learning process. Bruner reminded those critics who predict resulting anarchy from such an environment that subcommunal learning does not lessen a teacher's authorial voice. It merely allows her to add another voice—one that invites participation, encourages exchange, solicits alternatives.

I recall a watershed experience in college that illustrates the importance of delivery. I will never forget Mr. K. He was my collegiate second-

ary methods instructor. The course was one of the foundational education courses in my field and, despite its 8:00 a.m. time slot, it was filled
with eager, enthusiastic preteachers. Mr. K. would sit on his stool every
day for the entire class period and drone on and on about nothing of
consequence. We didn't have to take notes because his material came
directly from the text. He would wander off the subject and end up talking
at length about nonissues such as room acoustics. There was little dialogue with students, and when there was, it was filled with clichéd responses and an obvious discomfort with the subject matter and our demands for more depth. A five-week teaching practicum was associated
with this course. So there I was, an eager and enthusiastic college junior
who was totally unprepared for what would transpire on her first day with
a fifth-grade class . . . and with *Tracy*. When I entered the room, Tracy
was sitting in a garbage can. She refused to move when asked, responding with a surly "Make me, *bitch*." There I stood, completely frozen and
utterly demoralized by her rancor. We had not spent any time in class
learning to negotiate the treacherous territory of preadolescent behavior,
so I had no repertoire of responses. Frustrated, I went back to Mr. K,
pleading for some sort of guidance. He said that these things happen,
and with experience, I would eventually learn to cope.

Perhaps I should be grateful to Mr. K. That was a definitive moment in
time for me. It was the catalyst that led me to pursue a terminal degree. I
was *determined* to do a better job preparing young preservice educators
than he had done. I do not advocate that we *entertain* the troops, but we
do have to *engage* them. My advice is so laden with sense that it almost
seems too simplistic to include. Teach as you enjoy being taught. Ban the
podium. Move around the room. Make sustained and panoramic eye contact. Be articulate. Be impassioned. Say those well-prepared statements
with enthusiasm, vigor, and conviction. Participate fully and wholeheart-
edly in classroom debate and discussion. Be a performer—a person—a
pedagogue.

Raising the Bar

The axiom "those that can't, teach" has dogged our profession for de-
cades. To be truthful, some of my own Arts and Sciences colleagues
literally wrinkle their noses in disdain at the very mention of teacher education programs. As David Labaree said, "Teacher education came to be
perceived as every student's second choice and the ed school professors
came to be seen as second-class citizens in the academy."[39] We have

wittingly contributed to this perception by not upholding the last element of our pedagogical creed. We **must** raise the bar, propping it up on either side with two large placards—one that reads *Intellectual honesty resides here* and the other issuing the rallying cry, *Ban the banal.*

I've been thinking alongside Bruner for so many years that I hardly remember a time when I wasn't intellectually challenged by him. However, I do vividly remember which concept first struck a responsive chord in me—the idea of intellectual honesty. The notion that any subject can be taught to any child at any age in some form that is honest, interesting, and powerful must have appeared both comforting *and* terrifying to the post-Sputnik generation of educators. I've always thought that the Woods Hole Conference was a gigantic go-meta session. It was a chance for teachers, curriculum designers, and intellectual catalysts of that turbulent period to collectively catch their breath and calmly reaffirm the need to focus on the learning process (rather than merely the subjects to be taught). The participants called for reflection amid the push for more substantive content, intuitive thought alongside analytical exegesis, and a recommitment by teachers to deliver curricula that simultaneously changed, moved, perturbed, and informed both teachers and students.[40]

According to Bruner, presentations of material that are delivered in exciting, correct, and comprehensible ways require "deep understanding and patient honesty."[41] From my experience, the lack of intellectual honesty seems to involve assumptions that often err on the side of not enough. Let me explain. When we truly understand a subject (or discipline), we also have a sense of its structure from the simplest elements to the most complex and all the interrelationships between the variables. Bruner said that we are then faced with the dilemma of trying to communicate the idea without too much loss of precision and in a form where we can expand to include more detail at a later date.[42] This is the point where well-meaning teachers are often intellectually dishonest. They cannot communicate the material in an age or level-appropriate way, feeling the need to water down content for the learner to the point that it loses validity. As mentioned earlier, the concept of loud and soft volume or dynamic levels (with all of the inherent acoustical properties and explanations) can indeed be taught to individuals without much musical experience or a priori knowledge in a manner that upholds the accuracy of the principle. However, if in an effort to reach this population, I oversimplify the concept so that it loses accuracy or credibility in a later, more sophisticated learning episode, I have been intellectually dishonest. For example, I commonly witness young teachers equating *loud* with big or fast and *soft* with small or slow. This association might momentarily make a concrete connection but in more sophisticated musical contexts, the analogy breaks down. One might suggest that inaccuracies which are reinforced are easily corrected—no harm done. Bruner would argue that this kind of teaching lacks economy, and I would add, lacks a desirable ethical standard.

Ban the Banal

When I think of banality in both substance and style, I am reminded that we as teacher educators have surrendered, in a sense, to the "well, they are only education majors" syndrome. This is demonstrated by our tendency to keep lowering the bar, diluting standards, making allowances for mediocrity. I agree with Bruner that we owe it to students as a pedagogical courtesy to pace learning so that it is neither a burden or a bore.[43] One way we can address this is by the materials we choose to use.

Realistically, though, just how much thought and effort go into selecting the materials students will use in their methods courses? From my experience, not enough. Expediency is usually the deciding factor and woe to the brave individuals who decide to change the text(s) of a course that they have inherited. Instead of being commended for trying to initiate innovations and change, the effort is often met with skepticism and the "well-if-you-must" look.

We should make it a habit to continually be on the lookout for materials that

1. reflect and promote our own pedagogical value systems,
2. challenge the students' intellectual capabilities, and
3. provide a cutting edge view of the profession.

Pablum should not be tolerated.

I winced when I read a statement made by Seymour Papert in a recent issue of *Time*. The article was summarizing the contributions of Jean Piaget to twentieth-century psychology. Dr. Papert stated that "although every teacher in training memorizes Piaget's four stages of childhood development (sensorimotor, preoperational, concrete operational, formal operations), the better part of Piaget's work is less known, perhaps because schools of education regard it as 'too deep' for teachers."[44] What an embarrassing indictment if this is true! Are we choosing texts that tend to dumb down material? Do we choose the path of least resistance? Have we, as Ann Brown suggests, neglected to actively campaign for "mindful learning?"[45]

With all of the available technological resources, we should be able to easily locate texts that challenge the learner, that push their learning envelope. Adopting new materials, however, presupposes a willingness to grow and change our approach to any given course. The additional preparation time needed to become accustomed to new material is usually far outweighed by the pedagogical benefits.

Recently, a book I normally use for an exceptional learner class became unavailable (out of print). I liked this text so much that I tracked down the author. When we were unable to work out a compromise between reasonable photocopying costs and the author's profit margin, I began soliciting advice from colleagues in the field whose opinions I trusted and whose pedagogical value systems closely resembled my own. I took a text suggestion from one colleague, ordered the text, learned along with the students and, as a result, enhanced my knowledge base and energized and animated the course.

In an earlier piece, Bruner lamented the superficiality of the texts used with school-age children. He complained that basal readers were often stripped of both readability and a sense of passion as if children need to be shielded from the frailties of the human condition. Consider his opinion of one particular historical account:

> He [Columbus] was a man driven to explore, to control. The justification for the pablum that makes up such textbooks is that such accounts as these touch more directly on the life of the child. [Here Bruner describes an innocuous little conversation between a juvenile Christopher Columbus and his brother regarding the shape of the earth.] What is this "life of the child" as seen by text writers and publishers? It is an image created out of an ideal of adjustment. The ideal of adjustment has little place for the driven man, the mythic hero, the idiosyncratic style. Its ideal is mediocentrism, reasonableness above all, being nice. Such an ideal does not touch closely the deeper life of the child. It does not appeal to the dark but energizing forces that lie close beneath the surface. The Old Testament, the Greek myths, the Norse legends—these are the embarrassing chronicles of men of passion. They were devised to catch and preserve the power and tragedy of the human condition—and its ambiguity, too. In their place, we have substituted the noncontroversial and the banal.[46]

Doesn't that piece, written 30 years ago, seem to be describing the current political correctness scene? I'm concerned that political correctness has infiltrated Foundations of Education textbooks to the point where authors go to great lengths to avoid honest debate of the points of dilemma within our profession. Remember the soil/seed analogy from chapter 2? We should not be reticent about asking the tough questions—the tilling process depends on it.

What about educational software? Bruner commented in the early sixties about the lack of imagination of programmed texts (the "software" of the time). Their inability to engage the learner prompted him to encourage authors and publishers to "take as their model in programming the dialogue between Socrates and the slave boy in the market—and not the image of the pigeon pecking frenziedly at his key, waiting for a grain of corn."[47]

By extrapolation, we can say the same about contemporary educational software products. Here I must make a confession. Although my students learn to use various music and educational software packages in other classes, I have yet to see the need to incorporate these into the methods class. I would rather give them the electronic resources (and the opportunity to practice using them in context) that will enhance their research efforts, their problem solving capabilities, and their thirst for transfer. However, I limit cyberspace citations to approximately one-fourth of the total number of research references in scholarly papers. I still believe in the old-fashioned archeological dig. In my opinion, it engages and challenges the mind to a greater degree. Until proven otherwise, I'll continue this mix of technology and tradition.

Mentor Mentality

Finally, our role as teacher educators doesn't end when students graduate. Remaining a resource presence in our graduates' lives is vital to their continued success. While I'm hopeful that every teacher educator maintains a letters-from-the-heart file (notes of appreciation from former students), we need to do more than just receive their expressions of gratitude. The crux of the matter can be found in two words: be available. Be available to those young teachers during their first few years of teaching. While some public schools do a fair job of mentoring first-year teachers, others leave them alone to deal with impossible situations. Make it your business to track the job placement history of graduates and then keep in touch through the phone, fax, e-mail, visits . . . anything to make a connection. For example, for the past year I've been receiving and responding to correspondence from a former student who accepted a position in another state. I was primarily a sounding board as she navigated her way through the predictable highs and lows of first-year teaching. I had opportunities to praise her successes, recommend resources, and temper her overzealous and sometimes misplaced passion for justice. I like to think I filled an important role for her.

While at a recent professional conference, I had several former students find me. On the exhibit floor, en route to a session, in the bathroom—they would all appeal for a few minutes. Postponing plans to have coffee or to do lunch seemed like a small sacrifice once I listened to their concerns. Their gratitude for my words of advice and encouragement was embarrassing. I think I owe them as much.

We are in an age of increased accountability. In our state, there is a concerted effort to hold Colleges of Education accountable for the success/failure of their graduates. Many of my colleagues find this trend insulting or intimidating. I find it invigorating. Please—hold me accountable. If I have done my job, my students should find their ways with integrity, dignity, enthusiasm, and competence.

Notes

1. J. S. Bruner. (1965). The growth of mind. *American Psychologist, 20*, 1007.

2. J. S. Bruner. (1966). *Toward a theory of instruction.* Cambridge, MA: Belknap Press of Harvard University, 124.

3. J. S. Bruner. (1992). Science education and teachers: A Karplus lecture. *Journal of Science Education and Technology, 1*(1), 5.

4. J. S. Bruner. (1996). *The culture of education.* Cambridge, MA: Harvard University Press, 44.

5. J. S. Bruner. (1985). Models of the learner. *Educational Researcher, 14*(6), 5–6.

6. Bruner, *The culture of education,* 49.

7. Bruner, *The culture of education,* 54.

8. J. Bruner (personal communication, April 22, 1999).

9. Bruner, *The culture of education,* 54–56.

10. Bruner, *The culture of education,* 56–58.

11. D. N. Orlofsky. (1997). Going behind the notes. *Clavier, 36*(9), 9–11, 24.

12. J. Bruner (personal communication, April 22, 1999).

13. Bruner, *The culture of education,* 60–62.

14. Bruner, *The culture of education,* 63.

15. Bruner, *The culture of education,* 50.

16. J. S. Bruner. (1961). The act of discovery. *Harvard Educational Review, 31*, 32.

17. J. S. Bruner. (1979). *On knowing: Essays for the left hand.* Cambridge, MA: Harvard University Press, 82.

18. J. S. Bruner. (1960). On learning mathematics. *The Mathematics Teacher, 53*(8), 613.

19. Ideas from Heather Watkins, student in MUS 361 at Troy State University.

20. J. S. Bruner. (1963). Structures in learning. *NEA Journal*, 52(3), 27.

21. J. S. Bruner. (1965). The growth of mind. *American Psychologist, 20*, 1014.

22. Bruner, *Toward a theory of instruction,* 159.

23. D. Wood, J. S. Bruner, & G. Ross. (1976). The role of tutoring in problem solving. *Journal of Child Psychology, 17*(2), 91.

24. J. S. Bruner. (1985). On teaching thinking: An afterthought. In *Thinking and learning skills, volume 2: Research and open questions*. S. Chipman, J. Segal, & R. Glaser (Eds.). Hillsdale, NJ: Lawrence Erlbaum Associates, 604.

25. B. Shore. (1997). Keeping the conversation going: An interview with Jerome Bruner. *Ethos, 25*(1), 12.

26. Homer. (8th-century B.C.). The Odyssey (R. Fitzgerald, Trans.). In B. Wilkie & J. Hurt (Eds.), *Literature of the Western World* (pp. 254–573). New York: Macmillan Publishing Company, 321.

27. J. S. Bruner & E. Hall. (1970). Bad education—a conversation with Jerome Bruner and Elizabeth Hall. *Psychology Today, 4*(7), 57.

28. J. S. Bruner & B. Clinchy. (1966). Toward a disciplined intuition. In J. Bruner (Ed.), *Learning about learning: A conference report*. (ERIC Document Reproduction Service No. ED 015 492, pp. 71–83). Washington, DC: US Government Printing Office, 72.

29. Bruner, *The culture of education*, 37.

30. J. S. Bruner. (1966). The will to learn. *Commentary, 41*(2), 44–45.

31. J. S. Bruner. (1969). The relevance of skill or the skill of relevance (pp. 4–13). In Merle E. Meyer and F. Herbert Hite (Eds.), *The application of learning principles to classroom instruction*. The First Western Symposium on Learning: Western Washington State University, 8.

32. J. S. Bruner. (1971). The process of education revisited. *Phi Delta Kappan, 53*(1), 21.

33. Bruner, *The process of education*, 90.

34. J. S. Bruner. (1986). *Actual minds, possible worlds*. Cambridge, MA: Harvard University Press, 126.

35. Bruner, A Karplus lecture, 5.

36. Bruner, *The culture of education*, 64.

37. Bruner, *The culture of education*, 84.

38. J. S. Bruner. (1961). The act of discovery. *Harvard Educational Review, 31*, 23.

39. D. F. Labaree. (1999). Too easy a target: The trouble with ed schools and the implications for the university. *Academe, 85(1)*, 36.

40. Preface to *The process of education*, xv.

41. Bruner, *The process of education*, 22.

42. Bruner, On learning mathematics, 615.

43. J. S. Bruner. (1962). Books, courses, and curricula. In *The Challenge of Change* (pp. 3–10). New York: The American Textbook Publishers Institute, 7.

44. S. Papert. (1999, March 29). Jean Piaget. *Time, 153*, 105–107.

45. A. L. Brown. (1994). The advancement of learning. *Educational Researcher, 23*(8), 9.

46. J. S. Bruner. (1959). Learning and thinking. *Harvard Educational Review, 29*(3), 190.

47. Bruner, Books, courses and curricula, 6.

Bruner On . . .

Piaget

During our conversation in 1995, Bruner recalled his experience of wandering in the mountains with Jean Piaget, feasting together on stale bread. What a vivid picture that created for me—oh, to have been an eavesdropping mädchen. Piaget was some 20 years his senior and, while they often disagreed, it seems each had a healthy respect for the other's work.

The following excerpt, taken from his intellectual autobiography, reveals the unique relationship between Bruner and Piaget and the research that grew as a result of the association. The time was circa 1955–1956, and Bruner was at the University of Cambridge:

> It was also the time of my first visit to "Le Patron," Piaget, in Geneva. We struck it off very well. With Piaget, one can be as critical as one needs to be so long as one does not cast doubt on the underlying *approach* of his theory of development. Once a topic can be shown to be discussable in terms of that approach—can be shown, for example, to fit into his ideas about the conversion of sensorimotor into operative schema, or to fit the doctrine of equilibration, or the underlying logical structures of operational and formal intelligence—Piaget will argue hard, well, and with enormous good humor. In any case, he saw *A Study of Thinking* as a blow for the common cause and wrote me an enthusiastic and encouraging letter about it, and in turn I was becoming much more conversant with and enthusiastic about his latest theoretical writing. We walked for hours through the mountains, in deep conversation, picnicking off stale bread covered generously with mayonnaise pressed from a tube and mixed with freshly squeezed garlic clove, a garlic press being part of the standard ware inside his rucksack. He particularly delighted in predicting where snails were to be found and, finding them, noting the marvelous and invariant regularity of their shells. I teased him, suggesting that his theory of development might be too closely modeled on the snail and might not take full enough account of how different motivational and experiential conditions affect mental growth. He was amused and a little shocked. And so was I—in retrospect!

We shift the scene to the early 1960s and to Harvard University, where, under the direction of Bruner and George Miller, its Center for Cognitive Studies was prospering:

> For a psychologist interested in intellectual development in the 1960's, the start-ing point was Piaget. Rightly so, for his structuralist reformulation truly "reconventionized" and modernized psychology in our day. But his was a need-lessly quiescent account of development. As I read more Piaget, three points of dissatisfaction began to emerge. The first was his indifference to the *specific* history of an organism's experience. Whatever the child did, whatever he en-countered within very broad limits, the stages unfolded in their timeless, logical way. The environment, indeed, was simply *aliment*, which, in slang, is like our pablum. Second, the operative filter to experience was always stage-specific. Noth-ing could get past it save what conformed to the rules of organization of the particular "stage." Was there no way of tempting growth? Was there, in Marxist lingo, no liberating principle? And third, Piaget's central concept of equilibrium controlling the unfolding of stages struck me as so much hanky-panky. It seemed to me that there *were* forms of environmental "nutriment" that had more effect on growth than others and these somehow got through or under the filter.
>
>   . . . There followed a lively period of exchange between Geneva and Harvard, financed by Ford. Bärbel Inhelder spent a year at the Center and then there were visits back and forth with seminars. Piaget presided over his seminars and discus-sions with the somewhat slow and determined direction of a glacier. Data was presented by an *assistant*, always framed in a fashion to fit the logically defined topic of the year, and each year had its topic. "Le Patron" would then set forth the interpretation in a magisterial fashion comparable to a flawless Landowska per-formance of Bach's *Art of the Fugue*. It was breathtaking and brooked no major contradiction. If fundamental objections were raised, questioning the general *view-point*, they were handled with a rather withdrawn respect and put aside as out of the spirit of the logical framework. If within the framework, Piaget is a superb and totally engaged protagonist. His response is never "oppositional"; it is invariably to show, in ever more "logical" detail, how *his* argument handles all the phenom-ena necessary to it. It is a magnificent single-mindedness and, I think, lies at the root of his singular systematic thrust. But it is not easy to live with theoretically. He ingests everything offered, and it comes out more Genevan than ever.
>
>   . . . There were fruitful research spin-offs—particularly as regards the role of language in development, the role of conflict in stimulating development, and, particularly, the role of cultural factors in shaping the course of cognitive growth (principally, Patty Greenfield's contribution). But I feel that the theoretical thrust of the work as a whole came from Piaget. We dedicated the book to him.[1]

I recall well the lunch at the Ukrayina Hotel in Moscow at the International Con-gress in 1966 when we presented it to him officially. It was rather a stiff lunch, for he did not like the book. Roman Jakobson eased the occasion with a remarkable wit that can make light of any intellectual heresy. Piaget and I have not been very close since, though I keep a close working contact with Inhelder, Sinclair, and others there. For all that, the research and the book that came from it have had useful reverberations.[2]

Notes

1.   This refers to J. S. Bruner, R. R. Oliver, & P. M. Greenfield, et al. (1966). *Studies in cognitive growth: A collaboration of the Center for Cognitive Studies*. New York: Wiley & Sons.

2.   J. S. Bruner. (1980). Jerome S. Bruner. In G. Lindzey (Ed.), *History of psychology in autobiography*, Vol. 7 (pp. 75–151). San Francisco: W. H. Freeman, 114–115, 125–7.

Chapter Six

A Two-Way Street

Teaching and learning are no longer to be seen as two activities, causally linked—one knows X because one was taught X—but rather as one special form of sharing or coming to share beliefs, goals, and intentions—in a word, as a culture.[1]

Vito Perrone speaks of the mutuality of teaching in his book, *Letters to Teachers: Reflections on Schooling and the Art of Teaching.* Ying and yang, give and take occur when teachers know students' interests, learning patterns, methods of discovery (even their gestures), and when students reciprocate by knowing the interests, passions, reservoirs of knowledge, and levels of commitment of their teachers. The teaching/learning dynamic is, according to Perrone, a "fully human activity" that presupposes input from and benefit to all participants.[2]

We have discussed what the teacher educator should bring to the table. Now, let's turn our attention to the characteristics and qualifications, if you will, of the learner. Traffic flows in both directions in the teaching/learning paradigm. One of my undergraduates made this analogy: ". . . a couple was dating and the guy was always buying flowers, candy, and doing everything that he could to make [the relationship] better. All the girl did was complain. Finally one day, the girl said she was not 'feeling it,' and the guy replied, 'I can't start the fire by myself. You need to put some fuel on it, too!' The teacher-student relationship is like this couple."[3] Indeed, the contributions and responsibilities of the learner can't be overlooked or underplayed.

Building Communities

I've come to realize that in order for students to be independent learners, they must also be codependent learners. Now, while on the surface this might sound contradictory, codependency lies at the heart of any learning community. It also may be the missing link in many methods classrooms.

According to Bruner, a radical realignment of the classroom dynamic has emerged from a cultural-psychological approach to education. It purports a "subcommunity of mutual learners" where students help each other learn, capitalizing and utilizing the abilities, strengths, and predispositions each individual brings to the task. I love the term "scaffolding" that often accompanies this idea because it is loaded with visual significance. There is division of labor implicit in any community, and most assuredly in this subcommunity, learners share the load. Some act as record keepers, some as surveyors, others as encouragers, even as negotiators.[4] Words that are associated with learning communities, such as *participatory, proactive, communal,* and *collaborative,* describe learning environments where students construct meanings as opposed to merely receiving them.[5] As I mentioned in the last chapter, the teacher is not rendered obsolete but an equal partner in this hierarchy. Here instructors provide a leg-up for students. We no longer assume the role of pilot—rather we act as navigators.

Perhaps the time has come for us to change many of the traditions of the methods classroom and work to instill if not the letter, at the very least the spirit of this community dynamic. I keep returning to the fundamental question of *how.* I believe it goes beyond randomly assigning students to group projects or reports or dividing into smaller group discussion units. It involves an overhaul of our current mindset. We, the teachers, usually regard ourselves as all-knowing and the students as knowing little to nothing. Extend this line of reasoning and the resulting lack of regard for students' knowledge bases prohibits us from seriously considering our classroom as a community of learners. Plainly put, many of us don't think students can handle a participatory role and we wouldn't dream of stooping to enter a collaborative relationship with them. If we've reached impasse, then what are our options?

Bruner reminds us that the status quo is not very successful—and change, which will require our commitment to a new way of thinking, will be challenging at best.

> Our Western pedagogical tradition hardly does justice to the importance of intersubjectivity in transmitting culture. Indeed, it often clings to a preference for a degree of explicitness that seems to ignore it. So teaching is fitted into a mold in which a single, presumably omniscient teacher explicitly tells or shows presumably unknowing learners something they presumably know nothing about. Even when we tamper with this model, as with "question periods" and the like, we still remain loyal to its unspoken precepts. I believe that one of the most important

gifts that a cultural psychology can give to education is a re-formulation of this impoverished conception. For only a very small part of educating takes place on such a one-way street—and it is probably one of the least successful parts.[6]

Activities that stress a community of learners' mindset defy the "every man/woman for his/her self" mentality and encourage students to take academic responsibility for each other. Consider this attempt to transfer the communal approach to a methods class assignment. Traditionally in my secondary music methods class, each student is individually responsible for the conception and development of a 9-week high school music appreciation unit.

That is, until I became dissatisfied with the overall results, finding many of the units to be predictable and bland. The breadth of coverage was there, but missing were the moments of creative inspiration and splashes of curricular innovation. Now we regard this activity as we would a building project. The architectural plans for the unit are housed in a user-friendly text called *Course Design: A Guide to Curriculum Development for Teachers*.[7] I act as the contractor-on-site, and class members subcontract according to their individual skills, strengths, and predilections. For example, if Richard is well-organized and a competent writer, he assumes the role of recorder. Sarah loves research, so she scouts around for appropriate supplemental curriculum materials. Dan is verbally articulate, so he takes the role of discussion leader, and so on. All of this activity does not happen in a vacuum, but is an ongoing, in-class process that lasts as long as is necessary. Bruner even suggested a wrap-up session where the whole class is allowed to "go meta" on the process itself (i.e., what was good with it, what went wrong, how it could be improved, and so forth) in order to get a sense of the process at work. The finished product? A pedagogically sound and stimulating unit in which all students have had an integral and equal share in creating. My role is one of facilitator and, while the students have to adjust to the role shift, eventually they begin to look to each other for assistance and information as much (or more) than they do to me. It is amazing how they learn to "shore each other up" and to work toward the shared goal. I truly believe it gives them a sense of "commitment to the web of social reciprocity" within the context of a practical teaching/learning experience.[8] Here are some examples of the kinds of feedback I regularly receive from students about their collaborative learning experience:

> With all the long nights aside, I don't believe there was anything in my college experience as positive as the collaborative learning project that my group completed. . . . I feel the most wonderful aspect of this project was the fact that it

gave me a sense of what could happen in the true teaching environment. The opportunity to do some extended planning and unit creation was irreplaceable.

Another positive contribution that this particular project made was that it was done with the communion of many creative minds. As a solo endeavor, it wouldn't have been such a well-rounded final project. When you pull in 10 or so future educators with different strengths and weaknesses, you are given a much broader creative setting with tons of diverse experiences to pull from.[9]

At first, I was a little nervous having to work with everyone in the class—I usually like to work on my own and do things my own way. But, as we got going, I eventually opened up to the idea. I like how we were made to think on our own . . . we've probably gone [through] four years of college being told how to do everything.[10]

I actually enjoyed the learning experience in the end. I feel that I learned more from the experience than I would have [from] most any other learning situation. It has really opened my eyes to what I need to learn to be a real musician and teacher . . . I'm glad I had the chance to work with the talent that was in the group.[11]

I have utilized collaborative learning and mentoring in other contexts as well. In an effort to improve the pedagogical skills of piano majors, I developed a program that united each piano major with a young pianist from the community. In addition to their weekly period of collegiate keyboard instruction, every piano principal was paired with a middle- or high-school piano student of advanced beginner or intermediate playing ability. The college student met weekly with a younger peer for an additional lesson. Each had the opportunity to practice pedagogical techniques as they listened and responded to the younger colleague's pieces and, in turn, performed works-in-progress for the younger student. The majors were also required to keep a journal of their experiences.

The following term found them, not with younger pianists, but paired with a member of their peer group in a similar learning dynamic. The benefits of this program far outweighed the inevitable logistical problems. Self-monitoring one's progress on a musical instrument can be an isolating and lonely experience, and these collaborative links seemed to provide needed opportunities for feedback, encouragement, and reflection, as well as a chance to hone one-to-one teaching skills.

I shared this project with Bruner and asked for his feedback on the suitability of the application. His comments provide insight into the reciprocity of learning:

I love this one! I want to tell you right off that I learn as much (about the subject involved) from teaching it as from the lonely effort of trying to master it. I never feel I understand anything really well until I've had a chance to teach it (or share it). The intersubjective act gets my understanding beyond the fuzzy autistic stage of "just" understanding. But this is even more so when I can share it with a peer and get some discourse started. But then again, I sometimes have difficulty distinguishing the difference between peer and student. But maybe it's because I take as my criterion in both cases that my interlocutor—student and peer—can exchange views about the matter as their final step in "getting" what my telling was about.

I've never taught piano, but I can imagine the loneliness involved in getting performance to where you want it to be or where it *ought* to be. There is something about playing it for/with somebody that must make a huge difference, particularly for/with somebody who is also trying to master it. . . .

My only other relevant example is what happens to a sailboat racing crew that works together for a long time—as with a gang I used to race with to Bermuda every other year for over a decade. You lose track of what you yourself "know" and what the gang "knows" collectively. And it's not just the banal stuff of getting your interactive timing right either. And it's the more spooky because after a while it gets silent and voiceless—everybody knowing what's supposed to be when it's supposed to be. I understand that jazz ensemble improvisation is a little like that when the ensemble's been together long enough.[12]

I'm genuinely hooked on infusing elements of collaborative learning into the methods classroom and have even taken the concept "on the road," to see how different age groups respond to the process. In fact, at the time of this writing, I have just completed a language arts and music project with a local kindergarten class.[13]

There is something vital and organic about communities of learners that are "involved jointly in solving problems with all contributing to the process of educating each other."[14] I agree with Bruner that there is a pride that grows from the shared experience; the knowledge that each has played an integral part in "constructing meanings" rather than merely retrieving them. I hope the reader senses my excitement because collaborative learning has energized my teaching like few things ever have. I hope it's contagious.

The "C's" to Success—Anything But Average

There is a tantalizing symbiotic relationship that exists between the cultivation of an individual's level of academic independence and the codependence that is created in a learning community. I believe shared knowledge and experiences make more effective individual scholars, and the sharper the individual is, the greater his contributions will be to the learning community. So, let's turn our attention to the individual teacher-in-training and the necessary components for academic (and pedagogical) success.

Commitment

I find it difficult to understand why any student, particularly someone preparing to enter the field of education, would not be committed to the learning process. Maybe the disappointment I feel when I encounter preteachers who lack the will to learn is only exacerbated by my own personal background. No one ever had to force learning upon me. From my earliest memories until now, learning has been and continues to be an exhilarating experience. As a young child, I was so content to just sit and read that my mother threatened to blast me off the back steps during the summer months. "Go and play," she would urge. Even so, to me, reading was more fun than traditional recreation. It *was* my play and everything was fair game—history, literature, foreign language, music. Learning wasn't a chore, it was an oasis.

I still approach almost every learning opportunity eagerly with a voracious appetite for knowledge and understanding, and I guess I expect the same from my students. Granted, the will to learn is intrinsic and often difficult to quantify. As Bruner said, "its source and its reward is in its own exercise."[15] However, I believe professional education programs should consider denying entrance to those students who have not sufficiently demonstrated a predilection toward learning for learning's sake. This may sound harsh, but we perpetuate our problems when we tolerate a mediocre mindset toward the process of learning—one that carries with it implications for generations of learners.

My experience has been that when a few faculty members (and it is surprising how few) call for more rigorous entrance requirements, challenging, stimulating, and intellectual course content, meaningful teaching experiences, and tougher exit examinations, many university officials balk. I must admit that the following statement made by David Labaree regarding market pressures within Colleges of Education rings true:

> Education schools that try to increase the duration and rigor of teacher preparation by focusing more intensively on smaller cohorts of students risk leaving the bulk of teaching in the hands of practitioners who are prepared at less demanding institutions or who have not been prepared at all. In addition, such efforts run into strong opposition from within the university, which needs ed students to provide the numbers that bring legislative appropriations and tuition payments. Subsidies from the traditionally cost-effective teacher-education factories support the university's more prestigious, but less lucrative, endeavors. As a result, universities do not want their ed schools to turn into boutique programs for the preparation of a few highly professionalized teachers.[16]

The push for academic quality may seem futile in light of the prevailing and overriding control of market driven policy making, but there are some of us who will continue our quixotic attempts. How can you spot students with that special intuitive sparkle in their eyes? Well, we cannot expect to evaluate commitment on the basis of one entrance interview. In this context, words are indeed cheap. Nor are we talking about the mere assemblage of high grades. At many institutions, a high grade point average simply indicates that students have become astute at giving instructors what they want. There is, after all, a chasm of difference between knowing *about* a subject and knowing how to *apply* the knowledge. I can know *about* music in the abstract, theoretical sense without knowing *how to make* music. The former lacks validity and resonance without the latter.

Those of us dedicated to teacher training have to identify ways in which we can determine whether students have a penchant for reflective thinking, the desire to generalize from one learning situation to another, and the commitment to self-improvement. I will gladly work with students who demonstrate these qualities. I find it hard, however, to become motivated to mentor students who think they already possess everything they need to know or who downgrade the vocation of teaching (by enrolling in the major merely for the job security of teaching credentials).

Establishing some way of monitoring the learning trends that students have established in all of their classes (general studies included) prior to entrance to the professional education sequence is no easy task. Some universities now require students to assemble elaborate portfolios illustrating their potential for teaching. These are subsequently judged by a panel of qualified and (I hope) committed methods instructors. Because many institutions are being held accountable for the performance of their education graduates, a portfolio might be helpful in both the tracking process and in the evaluation of exit proficiencies.[17]

However, this is not a panacea nor should portfolio assessment lull us into complacency. We must take on an even more aggressive, proactive strategy in order to fill our ranks with the right stuff. We do not need the Holmes Partnership nor any other reform group to tell us that recruiting the best and brightest to the teaching field should be a priority. Nevertheless, how seriously do we take the challenge to get the good ones?

In 1969, Bruner underlined the difficulties inherent in teacher recruitment:

> I am aware of the problem of recruiting and training teachers. It is *the* great problem in education. We do *not* recruit our ablest people into education, indeed we do not even recruit a proportionate share of the ablest into education—particularly elementary education where the turning off begins and is most often completed.[18]

Is it too simplistic to ask the question "Why not?" Every article or discourse I read on teacher education reform issues clarion calls for deliberate recruiting efforts. Even so, few Colleges of Education have established practices and policies toward this end. If we are very honest with ourselves, we would have to admit that this is yet another extension and manifestation of the theory to practice gap. It is going to take roll-up-your-sleeves efforts on the part of education faculty to begin to make a difference in the area of recruitment. Lines of dialogue must be created and resulting quality face-time must occur between personnel in our Colleges of Education and target high school student groups, such as the Future Teachers of America, professional honor societies within individual disciplines, or even interested students attending university preview days. In order to reach out to potential teachers, we will need university support for scholarship money, administrative support for release time, and collegial support for the integrity and demands of pedagogy. To be truly effective, the team must work together. However, in the absence of that, individual teacher educators can begin to make contacts. Simplistic though it sounds, change often begins with a single vision, a lone vote, a crusade of one. Commitment seems to be a two-way street.

Competence
Suitable—adequate—proficient—capable. Call it by whatever adjective you desire. Competence is *easy* to identify, track, and measure. Moreover, it is sustained by its own existence. It is no surprise that we are interested in what we get good at.[19] We work best when we operate in a "personal domain of interest."[20] My brother-in-law is a highly competent master electrician who exists in this circle of competence. His early successes with basic wiring fed his growing interest in the field of electricity which, in turn, pushed him toward skill mastery. Watching him perform a complicated wiring job is like watching an intricate finger ballet.

We demand competence in our tradespeople, our physicians, our retailers . . . why not our core of preservice teachers? However, the truly competent teacher is a three-dimensional creature who is

1. competent in subject matter mastery,
2. competent in the use of learning theory, and
3. competent in the successful combination of numbers one and two to the student population.

No easy feat, but the drive for competence is absolutely essential. Its existence will motivate behavior. When the desire for competence is present, the individual will have to rely less and less upon external reinforcement to sustain behavior.[21] Individual responsibility, initiative, independence in decision and action, perfectibility of self—all of these will bubble to the surface and push the individual learner toward a higher level of competence.[22]

Most preservice teachers would probably admit to desiring competence, and most of them want to be good teachers. However, as we know, there is often a great divide between wanting and doing. Cliff Madsen and Terry Kuhn used the following illustration:

> How can one tell whether a student will be a good teacher? Is it possible to project future teaching effectiveness by analyzing what a student is doing now? A student may think: "I get to class about 70 percent of the time, but I'm going to be a 100 percent teacher," or, "I'm a C student, but I'm going to be an A teacher," or "There are lots of ways to teach that I've heard about in my required classes, but I won't know what I'm going to do in the classroom until I get there.". . . some students take four years to prepare themselves and at the end are ill prepared. Perhaps they assume no relationship between what they *are* doing (learning) and what they *plan to do* (teaching). Yet one must face the possibility that thoughts expressing a disparity between preparing to teach and actual teaching may represent an "intellectual game."[23]

I answer their questions in the affirmative. I believe you can (and should) judge future teaching effectiveness by present indicators. Red flags vigorously wave when I see a student who either lacks the drive toward competence or who fails to translate his well-meaning intentions into good, old-fashioned, hard (cognitive) work. Bruner described how he was involved with a group of individuals who combined their intense drives for competence with tangible and methodical actions. I wish that our preservice populations would show a fraction of this kind of initiative and quest for excellence.

> When I was a graduate student at Harvard, a group of us got together to form an informal seminar of our own to study together for "prelims" (the bone crusher

exam you have to take in the second year to qualify for "candidacy"). We decided
that the best way to do it was to assign topics to each member, each to prepare a
"paper" for the next session laying out the topic. It was an astonishingly talented
group of half a dozen. Those discussion sessions based on the individual papers
prepared amounted to one of the best learning experiences I've ever had. And
you know, I really believe that the so-called Cognitive Revolution was hatched in
those informal seminars—though the chicken didn't break out of the egg for maybe
a dozen years. Years later, Gordon Allport said to me that it was the most "independent minded and arrogant and effective group of graduate students he'd seen
in his long years at Harvard! And believe me, were we ever a "community of
learners!"[24]

Curiosity

There is no need to linger on the need for curiosity and subsequent discovery in the lives of our preteachers as the topic has been discussed in
chapter 5 (in context with the teacher educator). I believe curiosity and
the motivation to achieve competence are inseparable. Quite simply,
". . . curiosity is almost a prototype of the intrinsic motive. Our attention
is attracted to something that is unclear, unfinished or uncertain. We
sustain our attention until the matter in hand becomes clear, finished, or
certain."[25] My experience has shown that without the light of curiosity,
the student/teacher will be content to dwell in mediocrity and the status
quo. The sparks of curiosity invariably ignite the process of trying to find
out (heuristics of discovery), and the more one explores, problem solves,
and enjoys forays into discovery, the more one will be able to generalize
to new and equally as provocative tasks.[26] When I asked Bruner why the
light of curiosity seems to be missing in many undergraduates, he responded in the following way:

> It never was a very bright light, that light of curiosity, alas. And it's probably
> dimmed further by the sense of the complexity of the world: "how can I manage
> all THAT!" On the other hand, if you treat them AS IF they had the light at FULL,
> they often take you at your word and act accordingly. That's my only "trick" for
> good teaching: treat them as if they were great learners.[27]

To prove one's curiosity does not necessitate an exploratory excursion
to the Yukon! Scale is not the issue and, according to Bruner, the outcome will not be a guaranteed huge discovery.[28] We simply long to see
initiative. The kind that would motivate, for example, one of our caregivers
to rummage around for suitable activities/playgames to assist my two-
year-old in her acquisition of language skills. Or the kind that would drive
a preteacher to take extra classes to shore up an area of weakness/inter-
est, or the kind who would encourage the same student to adopt a pre-

school class for one year in order to develop her ideas and contribute to their arts education. No credit, no fanfare—just a driving need to know. Would that we all could discover (or perhaps rediscover) the Curious George that lurks inside us. Then we could fully appreciate that "there are few things so exciting as sensing where one is trying to go, what one is trying to get hold of, and then making progress toward it. The reward of mastery, not the assurance that someday you will make more money or have more prestige."[29]

Care

The exceptional teachers I know are passionate about learning. They have deep interests in some aspect of learning—history, literature, science. They are so steeped in this passion that they could manage well if all the textbooks, workbooks, and curricular guides that fill the schools suddenly disappeared. They see connecting points everywhere. It is not possible to take a walk with them without noting that they are almost always seeing around them possibilities for their students. They make particular note of books, insist on "checking out" libraries and museums, write down addresses of people and places. Schools need to promote and support passion of this kind.[30]

This kind of passion, as described by Perrone, can't truly be quantified, but its effects can be. Commitment . . . competence . . . curiosity— they are inexplicably bound together, and they seem to be possessed by individuals who care deeply about learning and children. However, let's approach this subject of passion with a noncynical wariness. I tend to have a knee-jerk reaction to the clichéd responses given to the question "why do you want to be a teacher." All too often the answer is "because I love kids."

Now that is a *good* reason, but is it the *real* reason? The thesis behind the opening discussion in the text *Contemporary Music Education* is this: Too many students have backed into teaching for good reasons, but since they are not based upon reality, the students eventually realize (often when it is too late to reasonably alter their course) that teaching is *not* for them. The authors go on to point out that "even though school is not what some prospective teachers want, they still *do* become teachers, discover that they do not like it, and become disenchanted, discouraged, or just bored. In this situation everyone suffers: teachers and students."[31]

The authors suggest some questions to help the preservice individual examine past behaviors in order to honestly assess their *raison d'etre*. These include the following:

Do I enjoy learning? Do I spend time with children when I have the opportunity? Does it excite me to share a new idea? Do I find myself trying to teach others? Do

I have some positive models in past teachers I can emulate? Have I ever been a successful scout leader, young people's leader or Sunday school teacher? Did I *enjoy* babysitting? Did I play "school" as a child? Am I positive with young people, especially younger siblings? Why am I really here?[32]

Caring has another dimension that, until recently, I had overlooked. When I asked one of our graduate students what he thought preservice teachers needed to bring to the table, he mentioned a basic care for oneself. The more I thought about his line of reasoning, the clearer the connection between a developing sense of passion and a grounded sense of self-worth seemed to be.

If knowledge is to be imparted, the student must feel that he or she is worthy of receiving that knowledge. Currently, part of my graduate work includes teaching some piano classes to undergraduate students. Even as I write, the struggles of one student in particular, come to mind. Though she sits in a college classroom, there are profound struggles with issues of self-worth and self-esteem that continue to inhibit her ability to learn. Such basic needs, unmet somewhere in her life, prevent her from learning and performing to the [level] of the other students. Before that student can learn, she must learn to feel worthy and comfortable with her own rights to receive that knowledge. As is the case with all good teaching, lots of positive affirmation and praise will help that student make strides toward her competence. However, the necessity of such basic human needs [isn't] unique to any one particular educational setting. At the core of all learning, whether in or out of the classroom, is a basic sense of self-worth.[33]

Contemplation

Martha Harris Wurtz once told me that really fine teaching requires reflection at 2 a.m.; self-examination in the moments before sleep; inner predawn monologues. Moments where pedagogical failures are analyzed and redesigned and where successes are briefly celebrated, then mentally catalogued for later use.

I think the following quote from Will Durant captures the essence of the art of contemplation:

Philosophy begins when one learns to doubt—particularly to doubt one's cherished beliefs, one's dogmas and one's axioms. Who knows how these cherished beliefs became certainties with us and whether some secret wish did not furtively beget them, clothing desire in the dress of thought? There is not real philosophy until the mind turns round and examines itself.[34]

We've talked at length in this text about metacognition or thinking about one's thinking. Whether you call it "self-conscious reflectiveness," "retrospection," "reflective intervention," or "going meta,"[35] the meaning remains the same. It is a cognitive process that is equal parts proactive and reactive. Or as Bradd Shore put it, going meta is a "dialectical orneriness with the hope of a synthesis and reconciliation at the end."[36] I liken the concept to riding a bike. Examine a bike upside down in motion and you see spinning tires, spokes, chains, pedals—all connected, turning in on itself. Right side up and united with a human rider, beauty in motion can now achieve speed, distance, and a destination. Going meta is not simply the mental equivalent of the upside-down bike, but the realized potential of well-tuned machinery and humanity.

We should have preservice classrooms that are filled with meta bicyclists—students who are thoughtful, reflective, and contemplative and are not afraid to spend the necessary cognitive energy to evaluate how they (and others around them) think and learn. Sometimes the students yearn to ride, but need a little prodding (or as Bruner good-naturedly put it, "a little plaguing, goading, disturbing"[37]). In the spirit of Alfred North Whitehead, I sometimes want to shout to the students that "the time has come for you to stop mentally bending over your desk . . . stand up and look around."[38] Get on the cognitive bicycle and enjoy the ride! You'll be amazed at what you'll see and where you'll end up!

The beauty of contemplation is that it provides perspective and empowerment. These are things preservice educators seem to want and something we all know that they desperately need. As Bruner stated:

> If he fails to develop any sense of what I shall call reflective intervention in the knowledge he encounters, the young person will be operating continually from the outside in—knowledge will control and guide him. If he succeeds in developing such a sense, he will control and select knowledge as needed. If he develops a sense of self that is premised on his ability to penetrate knowledge for his own uses, and if he can share and negotiate the result of his penetrations, then he becomes a member of the culture-creating community.[39]

If we could send our students to their inaugural teaching position so prepared, I would be satisfied. Wouldn't you?

Notes

1. D. R. Olson & J. S. Bruner. (1996). Folk psychology and folk pedagogy. In D. R. Olson and N. Torrance (Eds.), *The handbook of education and human development* (pp. 9–27). Cambridge, MA: Blackwell, 10.

2. V. Perrone. (1991). *A letter to teachers*. San Francisco: Jossey-Bass, 27.

3. S. Langford (personal communication, May 11, 1999).

4. J. S. Bruner. (1996). *The culture of education*. Cambridge, MA: Harvard University Press, 21.

5. Bruner, *The culture of education*, 84.

6. Bruner, *The culture of education*, 21.

7. G. J. Posner & A. N. Rudnitsky. (1997). *Course design: A guide to curriculum development for teachers* (5th ed.). New York: Longman.

8. J. S. Bruner. (1966). *Toward a theory of instruction*. Cambridge, MA: Harvard University Press, 127. Also personal communication, April 11, 1999.

9. K. Weidner (personal communication, February 4, 2000).

10. R. Glasscock (personal communication, August 2, 2000).

11. W. Burroughs (personal communication, August 5, 2000).

12. J. Bruner (personal communication, April 11, 1999).

13. D. N. Orlofsky & R. Lyda. (2000). Working together: A look at collaborative learning in two different settings. Manuscript submitted for presentation consideration.

14. J. S. Bruner. (1996). What we have learned about early learning. *European Early Childhood Education Research Journal, 4*(1), 15.

15. Bruner, *Toward a theory of instruction,* 127.

16. D. F. Labaree. (1999). Too easy a target: The trouble with ed schools and the implications for the university. *Academe, 85*(1), 36.

17. See M. Mertz's (1999) overview of portfolios in teacher education programs titled Using portfolios: Assessment, review, evaluation. *ATE Newsletter, 32*(3), 4–5.

18. J. S. Bruner. (1969). Notes on divisive dichotomies. In T. Holland and C. Lee (Eds.), *The alternative of radicalism: Radical and conservative possibilities for teaching the teachers of American's young children*, pp. 48–61. New Orleans, LA: Conference of the Tri-University Project (ERIC Document Reproduction Service No. ED 046 941), 61.

19. Bruner, *Toward a theory of instruction*, 118.

20. G. Hatano & K. Inagaki. (1987). A theory of motivation for comprehension and its application to mathematics instruction. In T. A. Romberg & D. N. Steward (Eds.), *The monitoring of school mathematics: Background papers, Vol. 2. Implications from psychology, outcomes of instruction* (Program Rep. No. 87–2, pp. 27–66). Madison: Wisconsin Center for Educational Research.

21. J. S. Bruner. (1979). *On knowing: Essays for the left hand.* Cambridge, MA: Harvard University Press, 92.

22. J. S. Bruner. (1966). The will to learn. *Commentary, 41*(2), 44.

23. C. K. Madsen & T. L. Kuhn. (1994). *Contemporary music education.* Raleigh, NC: Contemporary Publishing Company, 5–6.

24. J. Bruner (personal communication, April 12, 1999).

25. Bruner, *Toward a theory of instruction*, 114.

26. Bruner, *On knowing*, 94.

27. J. Bruner (personal communication, April 28, 1999).

28. Bruner, *On knowing*, 93.

29. J. S. Bruner. (1971). The relevance of skill or the skill of relevance. In M. E. Meyer and F. H. Hite (Eds.), *The application of learning principles to classroom instruction* (The First Western Symposium on Learning, October 1969, pp. 4–13). Western Washington State University, 12.

30. V. Perrone. (1991). *A letter to teachers: Reflections on schooling and the art of teaching.* San Francisco, CA: Jossey-Bass, 117.

31. Madsen & Kuhn, *Contemporary music education*, 4.

32. Madsen & Kuhn, *Contemporary music education*, 4–5.

33. A. Williams (personal communication, April 27, 1999).

34. W. Durant. (1953). *The story of philosophy.* New York: Simon and Schuster, 8.

35. Terms found in the following: *The relevance of education; Actual minds, possible worlds; The culture of education*; personal communication.

36. B. Shore. (1997). Keeping the conversation going: An interview with Jerome Bruner. *Ethos, 25*(1), 24.

37. J. Bruner (personal communication, March 29, 1996).

38. A. N. Whitehead. (1932). *The aims of education and other essays.* London: Williams and Northgate, 41.

39. J. S. Bruner. (1986). *Actual minds, possible worlds.* Cambridge, MA: Harvard University Press, 132.

Bruner On . . .

"Dream Killers"

The artist in me (and/or the child) loves whimsy and I enjoy the opportunity, on occasion, to venture beyond the bounds of empirical studies. I dabble in children's fiction and enjoy making theory to practice connections like the ones in this book. In fact, for three years, I was a regular columnist for *The National Forum*. I loved being able to write about the arts—sometimes dovetailing the theme of the column with the overall topic of the issue. One such column, in the *Origins* issue, provoked a strong written response (negative) from a reader and a delightful reaction from Bruner when I shared it all with him.

In order to place my critic's comments (and Bruner's) in context, I've taken the liberty to reprint my column here:

> When I learned that the theme for this issue was "Origins," my typical academic's response was to immediately consult the *Historical Anthology of Music*. Volume One of the anthology boasts of the inclusion of musical examples "from the beginning" through 1800. "The beginning" refers to examples of extant pieces that have survived, usually in fragments, through the millennia. The *Anthology* begins with a Chinese Entrance Hymn for the Emperor that dates circa 1000 B.C. and quickly moves through ancient Japanese, Siamese, Hindu, Arabian, and Jewish fragments. The next example, and by far the most complete, is the famous First Delphic Hymn. This is one of 20 Greek pieces to have survived and dates circa 138 B.C. From there the *Anthology* moves into early Gregorian chant, and the rest, as they say, is history . . . at least music history.
>
> Then I pulled out Plato and read some of his penetrating arguments about the nature and place of music in the educational scene and in life in general. Both excerpts are from *The Collected Dialogues of Plato*.[1]
>
> . . . so much of music as is adapted to the sound of the voice and to the sense of hearing is granted to us for the sake of harmony. And harmony, which has motions akin to the revolutions of our souls, is not regarded by the intelligent

votary of the Muses as given by them with a view to irrational pleasure, which is
deemed to be the purpose of it in our day, but as meant to correct any discord
which may have arisen in the courses of the soul, and to be our ally in bringing
her into harmony and agreement with herself, and rhythm too was given by them
for the same reason, on account of the irregular and graceless ways which prevail
among mankind generally, and to help us against them . . .

. . . that education in music is most sovereign, because more than anything
else rhythm and harmony find their way to the inmost soul and take strongest
hold upon it, bringing with them and imparting grace, if one is rightly trained,
and otherwise the contrary?

How scholars have pieced together the "origins" of music is fascinating
stuff for musicologists, serious musicians, and lovers of history. However,
it suddenly seemed so arcane to me. Perhaps it is because I spend so
much time as an educator instructing would-be teachers about elementary music. Or perhaps it is because, as a mother of a toddler, I live
immersed in the musical strains of "I-love-you/you-love-me" and other
such Barneyisms. Either way, I felt a need to connect to a more rudimen-
tary view of the origins of music. I wanted to hear simpler even more
fanciful explanations on how music came to be. And I know from my
years as an elementary teacher, when it's originality you want, check with
the kids.

So, I asked the music teacher of my niece's fifth-grade class at Northville
Elementary School in New Milford, Connecticut, to pose the question
"where did music come from." The responses Mrs. Dombal received
seemed to group into three camps. Students imagined that music came
from African-Americans, Indians, or cavemen and cavewomen (even fifth-
graders are trying to be politically correct). It is interesting to see how
their fifth-grade understanding of origins does *not* include the Greeks—
perhaps if we included this era in the elementary curricula, our college
students wouldn't turn up their noses at the *Iliad* or give us that quizzical
"I-don't-have-a-clue" look during the *Odyssey*. Just a thought . . . however inaccurate and naive the fifth-graders viewpoints are, they are unde-
niably fresh, sincere, and worth hearing. Some of the best are recounted
here verbatim (original spelling preserved, also):

I think Indians started music with instruments with sticks, rocks and other
sources. Then maybe cavemen and women added the words and it caught on
(Lauren).

I think music was started as communication. I think cavemen used music
like phones (no name).

I think music started from noises that animals made. Then cave people hit
things together and they created noises with patterns. They devolped ways to

make it higher and it evolved and when they devolped languages they added
songs to it and it evolved to instrauments and kept evolving (Sean).

I think music was originated by Africa Americans. The Africa Americans
would make the instruments with wook. When they were brought to North
America as slaves they taught the indians, spanish, english, and french how
to play them (Jessie).

I think music was started by the Indians. The Indians would take bamboo
and carve it into a flute. The Indians would also use animal skins for drums.
When settlers came to America, the Indians would share their instruments.
Later they started singing and putting words with rhythm. Soon after they
started with metel instruments (Jennifer).

Music originated when Indians came. They praised the Lord. Eventually
that came to music (Andrew).

I think music got started with the cavemen and cavewomen. They said
words fast and it mad music. They would take things and bang them together
or blow something and that would make music too (Jenna).

My favorite fifth-grade response came from another fellow named
Andrew. He simply said, *I think music came from mothers . . . they*
sang songs to their children. The children wrote the songs down. And
not to be outdone, my other niece, who is a first-grader, wanted to put in
her two cents. She said that music came from the angels and they got it
from God.

I think I'll go and put up my *Historical Anthology of Music.* I'll reshelve
Plato for another day. I'd rather listen to the birdsongs or to the spontane-
ous melodies that spring from inside my daughter . . . and keep won-
dering. Wouldn't you?[2]

Being a teacher, I love getting inside the heads of kids in order to find
out how they view their world. These narratives were fanciful and imagi-
native and amusing. I thought they would be taken in the spirit in which
they were presented. Wrong. They elicited a diatribe of "What a sham,"
"How could a respectable journal like yours encourage such drivel and
inaccuracies," and so on. These written comments came from a musi-
cologist who, for some reason, could not participate in the wonderful life
of the mind of these children. No one likes criticism, but I was startled by
his lack of understanding and the rancor in his response. It is one thing to
refuse to come along for the ride and quite another to vilify the ancient
voices of children (to borrow from George Crumb).

However, Bruner lives the life of the mind and participates in the narratives of many individuals (children included) so I took great comfort in
his response:

There must be some way of blessing the dream killers and pedants, but it always escapes me when I'm face to face with them. They hate playing—playing in all its senses; listening to kids and Aeonian harps, stealing a kiss, skipping flat stones on still ponds, improvising to make it sound like Satie, even trimming a cat's whiskers a little to see whether that'll keep them from going through the narrow spaces (like my sister, Alice, once did and got her bottom bashed by my mother for it). Send your pedant-correspondent a puzzle like "Bach is to Mozart as Hobbes is to Hume—why?"

I had a funny thing happen the other day. A guy (serious) was doing research on who had "influenced" whom in the "mind sciences." He began with Nelson Goodman, the philosopher, who answered that I had influenced him. So this guy writes to ask me who'd influenced me. So I e-mailed back that Nelson Goodman had. And I kept thinking, as I enjoyed my tongue stuck to my cheek, "That'll fix him." And I think of the lovely touchy-feely Michelangelo throwing a wet sponge against the wall to yield up an idea for a picture. The origin of music? Bosh. It must have taken thousands of years for anybody to recognize that what they were making deserved a special name like "music." Music got "invented" in retrospect. "Hey, let's call that thing birds do, that you do with your voice when you're threshing, what they do when they're dancing—let's call it ALL music." "Hey, what a smashing name for it." Never would it have occurred to me that it was a "something." Such fun these pedants are.[3]

Notes

1. Both of these selections can be found in context within Edith Hamilton and Huntington Cairn's edition of *The Collected Dialogues of Plato* (published by Princeton University Press, 1961, pp. 1175, 646).

2. D. Orlofsky. (1996). Cavemen used music like phones. *The National Forum, 76*(1), 7–8.

3. J. Bruner (personal communication, April 17, 1996).

Chapter Seven

Finding Middle Ground

Recently, I was thumbing through several educational journals, searching for an article I needed to reference. After a few minutes of scanning titles, I felt my eyes glaze over. Once the article was found, I couldn't help shaking my head. I am a researcher and an academic, and many of these research reports struck *me* as removed, self-indulgent, and arcane. My criticism doesn't focus on quality; they were (for the most part) well-crafted and well-executed papers and were featured in prestigious and well-respected periodicals. Nor am I advocating an end to systematic examinations of the microscopic aspects of the profession. Quite the contrary. We need to continue to mend the split between the "world of knowledge" and the "world of pedagogy."[1] However, as Bruner reminds us, "Education—and education research—cannot be kept separate from the life of the culture at large."[2]

This incident merely served to remind me that practicing teachers often shrug their shoulders and mutter about the impracticality of educational research. They contend that it is not worth the effort required to wade through academic jargon in order to distill tidbits of information—information that will not likely affect day-to-day classroom life or the pedagogical and behavioral challenges that they face.

Theory to Practice

As a result there is the classic theory to practice divide: Scholars label inservice teachers shallow and uninformed; teachers call scholars removed and out-of-touch. Amazingly, when educational researchers are contributing to the rift, it becomes a split *within* the family, and those are often the most resistant to healing. Maher and Tetreault offer a possible explanation:

> Why does this division exist? One factor contributing to it is the view, held by many people, that knowledge is a disinterested search for universal truth, one

that is disassociated (sic) from the circumstances under which it is produced. Pedagogy, which focuses mainly on the process of attaining knowledge, is thus cut off from the enterprise of knowledge production. This separation, embedded in the organization of colleges, universities, graduate schools, and even graduate schools of education, denies the evolving nature of knowledge and the role of teachers and students in its ongoing constructions. Yet to explore how a given field is constructed and continually "made" by researchers, teachers, and students need not dilute content so much as contextualize it. For us, the term "pedagogy" applies not just to teaching techniques but to the whole classroom production of knowledge; it encompasses the full range of relationships among course materials, teachers, and students. Such broadened conceptualizations of pedagogy challenge the commonly held assumptions of the professor as a disinterested expert, the content as inherently "objective" and the method of delivery as irrelevant to the message.[3]

However, the theory to practice dilemma is not only found between the covers of academic journals. There has been plenty of criticism aimed at teacher education programs for this very problem and not without cause. If there weren't kernels of truth in the accusations, Colleges of Education wouldn't be constantly scrambling to reinvent themselves, hastily assembling K–12 collaborations in order to present a feet-firmly-planted-in-reality facade to their critics. Linda Darling-Hammond (at this writing, the executive director of the National Commission on Teaching and America's Future) described the theory to practice gap in an honest, direct way:

Shoehorning unintegrated courses into the four-year undergraduate program has created unhappy trade-offs between deep learning in a disciplinary field and serious understanding of teaching and learning. Teachers have often been taught to teach in lecture halls from professors who have not themselves ever practiced what they teach. Courses on subject-matter topics have been disconnected from courses on learning and development.

Most students have completed this course work before beginning student teaching, which usually consists of an eight-to-twelve week bout in a classroom of a teacher chosen as often for reasons of convenience or local politics as for demonstrated expertise. This brief clinical experience, appended to the end of the program, has offered few connections with what came before. Because university and school-based faculty members have typically not planned or taught together, many education students have encountered entirely different practices from those they studied in the university. When these new teachers have entered their own classrooms, they have rarely been able to remember or apply what they had learned in their courses. Thus, they reverted to what they knew best: the way they themselves had been taught.[4]

So, why is finding a suitable middle ground between theory and practice so difficult? I think part of the answer lies in the community of learner concept. The traditional approach finds the preservice teacher handed from methods teacher to methods teacher. I guarantee that most teacher educators rarely, if ever, attempt to dovetail or coordinate their classes in order to maximize sequence, effect compatibility of content, or coordinate teaching experiences. It has been my experience that methods instructors regard each other through a haze of skepticism, feeling that they have to safeguard their turf. Discourse is rare. We *should* be a model community of learners, seizing *every* opportunity to put our collective heads together, to share ideas and information, to cook up new and exciting pedagogical schemes. Sadly, this is not the case.

We then hand our preservice students over to their cooperating teachers for internship. This is also a misnomer. Do we *ever* really cooperate? Does the teacher educator ever offer to trade places with the cooperating teacher to truly experience the clinical setting that the intern will be required to maneuver? No, we swoop down for two or three visits of an hour or so, pass judgment on the intern, exchange niceties with the cooperating teacher, and leave, then we wonder why the system isn't functioning at its peak?

Again, I think the responsibility for narrowing "the gap between knowledge locked up in the university library or the scholar's mind and the face being taught in schools" lies with us.[5] In truth, teacher educators are the middle ground. We work with learning principles and the development of children on a daily basis and have (or should have) a firm grasp of current research trends. We are then in a position to move outside university walls and work with the practitioner on converting theoretical concepts into curricular applications.[6]

Without sounding overly simplistic or naive, collaboration takes place . . . one classroom at a time. Each public or private school classroom composite is unique and, to truly effect change, we must spend quality time *in* the classroom, being a student of its nuances and dynamics. If we really want to effectively bridge the theory to practice gap, however, we cannot go into the schools with a "I'm-the-great-and-powerful-Wizard-of-Oz-hear-me" attitude. I believe we have to start at the entry level. Let me give an example. Last year, I offered my services to our local elementary school every Wednesday morning. Not as a teacher educator or university academic, but as a mom. Pure and simple. My request was that they place me anywhere, doing anything that they needed. Cutting stencils, assembling portfolios, putting up bulletin boards, grading papers, helping struggling readers, working with small groups, acting as hall monitor. I needed to experience the rhythm of the institution in order to build an atmosphere of trust with the inservice practitioners. Only from this position of trust could I ever expect to establish meaningful dialogue and develop mutually beneficial projects.

Other activities that can help bridge the gap include:

- Offering my services as a curriculum or inservice consultant for new or struggling programs
- Volunteering to guest teach
- Bringing inservice teachers to my methods classroom and bringing my classes to them
- Requiring my students to participate in a "Make a Difference" program where they adopt a child, group of children, or class and spend weekly time assisting, mentoring, teaching, making connections with the kids (above and beyond other classroom teaching requirements)
- Role playing during every peer-to-peer teaching episode
- Planting various behavior problems during peer-to-peer teaching in order to assist preservice teachers in hands-on practice dealing with behavioral-crisis management, and conflict resolution
- Searching for ways to assist or build specific programs (such as arts education projects)
- Having a regular and positive dialogue with school administrators, brainstorming university/school partnership opportunities

I am by no means a paragon of collaborative virtue. Frankly, sometimes I would like nothing better than to hide away in my office, answering to no one but myself and my own scholarly pursuits. My contributions are simple, amateur, small-scale attempts—do they really make a difference in the overall scheme of pedagogy? I have to believe they do, particularly if *armies* of teacher educators were to become serious about collaboration in their own fashion.

I am encouraged by the success stories being generated by larger, wholesale K–16 collaborations. There are K–16 programs scattered throughout the country, but the concept has a long way to go before it is standard operating procedure in teacher education programs.[7] Until then, we must fill the void with missionary-like vision and zeal.

The Spirit of Woods Hole

However, the theory to practice bridge can't be built exclusively by the hands of teacher educators. We need to revisit the spirit of Woods Hole and continue to nourish collaborative efforts that extend across disciplines. As history reminds us, the perceived crisis in science education during the post-Sputnik era ignited the mutual concern of educators, psychologists, historians, biologists, physicists, and mathematicians. Bruner served as the chair of this historic collaboration, the results of which were chronicled in *The Process of Education*.

When I examined a draft copy of *The Process of Education*, I noticed marginalia that read "separation of scientist and scholar from teaching," and "psychology divorced from schools."[8] Bruner was concerned that the scientific community (or by extrapolation, the artistic community, the psychological community, the linguistic community, and so on) operated in spheres so far removed from educational circles that there was never any possibility of intersection. These people were excellent resources for curriculum design and content suggestions, and they remained virtually untapped. The situation has not significantly improved in the 40 years since Woods Hole. Although they may not be as plentiful as in the era of educational reform, grant monies do still exist for these kinds of collaborative efforts. We can't cry poverty. We can, however, lament over the lack of committed individuals to initiate and execute these efforts.

In 1965, Bruner expressed concern that psychology should assume a more proactive role in "the design of methods of assisting cognitive growth," whether that be through the development of educational toys, curricula, or merely the enrichment of the infant/preschool environment.[9] I think this level of involvement should extend further than the listing of a psychology consultant at the end credits of educational television programs geared to the preschooler. Those who know should go.

I've seen this kind of face-to-face collaboration work with composer-in-residence programs. The composer commits to a school for a certain length of time (long enough to see musical yields) and works with the children on the manipulation of the elements of music, compositional techniques, improvisatory skills, while composing pieces of music tailored to the specific school population (with an eye toward having the students perform the finished product). Everyone wins in this situation. The kids get a bird's eye view of the demands and rigors of artistry, the benefits of expert guidance, the satisfaction and aesthetic pleasure of discovery and performance while they are simultaneously developing appreciation and listening skills (that will make them musically literate adult consumers). We won't even go into the rewards for the composer. Kids have a way of providing inspiration, instruction, and insight well beyond their years.

Long before "it takes a village" became a feel-good cliché, Bruner applied the intent of the phrase to education:

> The psychologist cannot alone construct a theory of how to assist cognitive development and cannot alone learn how to enrich and amplify the powers of a growing human mind. The task belongs to the whole intellectual community: the behavioral scientist and the artists, scientists, and scholars who are the custodians of skill, taste, and knowledge in our culture. Our special task as psychologists is to convert skills and knowledge to forms and exercises that fit growing minds—and it is a task ranging from how to keep children free from anxiety and how to translate physics [insert your own discipline] for the very young child into a set of playground maneuvers that, later, the child can turn around upon and convert into a sense of inertial regularities.[10]

So, in memory of the spirit of Woods Hole, I challenge the intellectual community to roll up their collective sleeves and start making connections that will have an impact on a generation of learners.

Reflections

I have said nothing in the pages of this text that will be considered revolutionary or that will turn the pedagogical world upside-down. Nevertheless, the observations have been genuine, based upon my years as a teacher educator and an individual in pursuit of honest academic excellence and thoughtful reflection.

It should be obvious to most that Bruner's voice and influence has had a profound effect on the development of my educational philosophy. For that I make no apologies. Alison Gopnik once said: "[Bruner] has been a sort of intellectual Johnny Appleseed, leaving behind orchards of ideas. He has leapt and flown himself, but he has also enabled others to leap and fly after him."[11] For the flight, I offer my sincere gratitude.

Bottom line? Bruner loved, and still loves, teaching. He once confessed that he never longed for a pure research job—one that would rob him of that pleasure. He enjoyed "the hooking of others on problems that move me."[12] He delighted in undergraduates, graduates, and postdocs. The pedagogue in me smiles at this type of sustained enthusiasm for the art of teaching.

It seems fitting that I should end echoing Bruner's sentiments. In a letter written to Dr. William Kessen, he said:

> . . . basically, I think that perhaps in the long run, finding out something that is powerfully obvious may serve the end of change better. So I shall go on being a professor. Indeed after seven or eight years of hurly burly, I rather look forward to

the next seven or eight of not having to convince anybody of anything, not even virtue. . . . Maybe the brief contribution of Bruner and Skinner is that they make it possible for agents around here to consider education as a problem. If that *is* so, then I shall be quite content.[13]

I, too, will remain a professor of teacher education. I, too, hope to produce students who will question and redefine education through thought and action. In doing so, they will positively influence classrooms full of kids for years to come. That's all the pedagogical legacy I want.

Notes

1. F. Maher & M. K. Tetreault. (1999). Knowledge versus pedagogy: The marginalization of teacher education. *Academe, 85*(1), 40.

2. J. S. Bruner. (1999). Some reflections on education research. In E. C. Lagemann & L. S. Shulman (Eds.), *Issues in Education Research: Problems and Possibilities* (pp. 399–409). San Francisco: Jossey-Bass Publishers, 408.

3. Maher & Tetreault, 40–41.

4. L. Darling-Hammond. (1999). Educating teachers: The academy's greatest failure or its most important future? *Academe, 85*(1), 30–31.

5. J. S. Bruner. (1983). *In search of mind.* New York: Harper and Row, 180.

6. J. S. Bruner. (1963). How we learn and how we remember. *Harvard Alumni Bulletin, 66*(4), 166.

7. For information on K–16 collaborative efforts, see the article by L. Darling-Hammond (endnote 4) and S. Feldman. (1999). Only connect: Professors and teachers with a common mission. *Academe, 85*(1).

8. Marginalia on draft copy of *The Process of Education* is housed in the Harvard University Archives, HUG 4242.40.

9. J. S. Bruner. (1965). The growth of mind. *American Psychologist, 20*, 1010.

10. Bruner, The growth of mind, 1015.

11. A. Gopnik. (1990). Knowing, doing, and talking: The Oxford years. *Human Development, 33*, 338.

12. J. S. Bruner. (1980). Jerome S. Bruner. In G. Lindzey (Ed.), *History of psychology in autobiography,* Vol. 7, pp. 75–151. San Francisco: W. H. Freeman, 147.

13. J. S. Bruner. Handwritten letter to Dr. William Kessen, Yale University, dated March 12, 1966. Letter housed in the Harvard University Archives, HUG 4242.75.

Bibliography

Selected Works of Jerome S. Bruner

Bruner, J. S., & Postman, L. (1949). Perception, cognition, and behavior. *Journal of Personality, 18*, 14–31.

Bruner, J. S. (1950). Social psychology and group processes. *Annual Review of Psychology, 1*, 119–150.

Bruner, J. S. (1951). Personality dynamics and the process of perceiving. In R. R. Blake and G. V. Ramsey (Eds.), *Perception: An approach to personality*. New York: Ronald Press.

Bruner, J. S., Matter, J., & Papanek, M. L. (1955). Breadth of learning as a function of drive level and mechanization. *Psychological Review, 62*, 1–10.

Bruner, J. S., Goodnow, J. J., & Austin, G. A. (1956). *A study of thinking*. New York: Wiley & Sons.

Bruner, J. S. (1957). Going beyond the information given. In H. Gruber, et al. (Eds.), *Contemporary approaches to cognition: A symposium held at the University of Colorado*. Cambridge, MA: Harvard University Press.

Bruner, J. S. (1958). *Cognitive processes in learning blocks* (First Progress Report to United States Public Health Service, Grant 1324). Cambridge, MA: Harvard University, Laboratory of Social Relations.

Bruner, J. S. (1958). A colloquy on the unity of learning. *Daedalus, 87*(4), 155–165.

Bruner, J. S., Mandler, J. M., O'Dowd, D., & Wallach, M. A. (1958). The role of over-learning and drive level in reversal learning. *Journal of Comparative and Physiological Psychology, 51*, 607–613.

Bruner, J. S. (1959). Learning and thinking. *Harvard Educational Review, 29*(3), 184–192.

Bruner, J. S. (1960). On learning mathematics. *The Mathematics Teacher, 53*(8), 610–619.

Bruner, J. S. (1960). The functions of teaching. *Rhode Island College Journal, 1,* 2ff.

Bruner, J. S. (1960). *The process of education.* Cambridge, MA: Harvard University Press.

Bruner, J. S. (1961, June 17). After John Dewey, what? *Saturday Review,* 58–59, 76–77.

Bruner, J. S. (1961). The act of discovery. *Harvard Educational Review, 31,* 21–32.

Bruner, J. S. (1962). Books, courses and curricula. In *The challenge of change* (pp. 3–10). New York: The American Textbook Publishers Institute.

Bruner, J. S. (1962). *On knowing: Essays for the left hand.* Cambridge, MA: Harvard University Press.

Bruner, J. S. (1963). How we learn and how we remember. *Harvard Alumni Bulletin, 66*(4), 163–166, 180.

Bruner, J. S. (1963). [Learning project and President's Panel on Education, Research and Development]. Handwritten notes, Jerome S. Bruner Papers, Harvard University Archives.

Bruner, J. S. (1963). Looking at the curriculum. *The Educational Courier* (Toronto), *33,* 18–26.

Bruner, J. S. (1963). Structures in learning. *NEA Journal, 52*(3), 26–27.

Bruner, J. S. (1964). Education as social invention. *Journal of Social Issues, 20*(3), 21–33.

Bruner, J. S. (1964). Is well begun half done? *New Directions in Kindergarten Conference.* Cambridge: Lesley College.

Bruner, J. S. (1964). On teaching teachers. In G. Kerry Smith (Ed.), *Undergraduate education: 1964 current issues in higher education.* Washington, DC: Association for Higher Education.

Bruner, J. S. (1964). The course of cognitive growth. *American Psychologist, 19*, 1–15.

Bruner, J. S. (1965). Liberal education for all youth. *The Science Teacher, 32*(8), 19–21.

Bruner, J. S. (1965). The growth of mind. *American Psychologist, 20*, 1007–1017.

Bruner, J. S. (1966). The will to learn. *Commentary, 41*(2), 41–46.

Bruner, J. S. (1966). Theorems for a theory of instruction. In J. S. Bruner (Ed.), *Learning about learning: A conference report.* (ERIC Document Reproduction Service No. ED 015 492, pp. 196–210). Washington, DC: U.S. Government Printing Office.

Bruner, J. S. (1966). *Toward a theory of instruction.* Cambridge, MA: Harvard University Press.

Bruner, J. S., & Clinchy, B. (1966). Toward a disciplined intuition. In J. S. Bruner (Ed.), Learning about learning: A conference report (ERIC Document Reproduction Service No. ED 015 492, pp. 71–83). Washington, DC: U.S. Government Printing Office.

Bruner, J. S., Oliver, R. R., & Greenfield, P. M., et al. (1966). *Studies in cognitive growth: A collaboration of the Center for Cognitive Studies.* New York: Wiley & Sons.

Bruner, J. S. (1968). *Processes of cognitive growth: Infancy.* Worcester, MA: Clark University Press and Barrer Publishers.

Bruner, J. S. (1969). Eye, hand, and mind. In D. Elkind and J. H. Flavell (Eds.), *Studies in cognitive development: Essays in honor of Jean Piaget.* New York: Oxford University Press.

Bruner, J. S. (1969). Notes on divisive dichotomies. In T. Holland and C. Lee (Eds.), *The alternative of radicalism: Radical and conservative possibilities for teaching the teachers of America's young children* (pp. 48–61). New Orleans, LA: Conference of the Tri-University Project (ERIC Document Reproduction Service No. ED 046 941).

Bruner, J. S., & Hall, E. (1970). Bad education—A conversation with Jerome Bruner and Elizabeth Hall. *Psychology Today, 4*(7), 50–57.

Bruner, J. S. (1971). Overview on development and day care. In E. H. Grogberg (Ed.), *Day care: Resources for decisions*. Washington, DC: Office of Economic Opportunity.

Bruner, J. S. (1971). The perfectibility of intellect. In A. R. Desai (Ed.), *Essays on modernization of underdeveloped societies, 1*. Bombay: Thacker & Co.

Bruner, J. S. (1971). The process of education revisited. *Phi Delta Kappan, 53*(1), 18–21.

Bruner, J. S. (1971). *The relevance of education*. New York: W.W. Norton and Company.

Bruner, J. S. (1971). The relevance of skill or the skill of relevance. In M. Meyer & F. H. Hite (Eds.), *First Western Symposium on Learning* (pp. 4–13). Bellingham, WA: Western Washington State University.

Bruner, J. S. (1973). On the continuity of learning. *Saturday Review of Education, 1*(2), 21–24.

Bruner, J. S. (1974). Child's play. *New Scientist, 62*(694), 126–128.

Bruner, J. S. (1974). Patterns of growth (Inaugural Lecture at Oxford University, May 25, 1973). Oxford: Clarendon Press.

Bruner, J. S. (1975). The role of the researcher as an adviser to the educational policy maker. *Oxford Review of Education, 1*, 183–188.

Bruner, J. S. (1976). Surprise, craft and creativity. In J. S. Bruner, A. Jolly, & K. Sylva (Eds.), *Play—Its role in development and evolution* (pp. 641–642). New York: Basic Books.

Bruner, J. S. (1976). The styles of teaching. *New Society, 36*(708), 223–225.

Wood, D., Bruner, J. S., & Ross, G. (1976). The role of tutoring in problem-solving. *Journal of Child Psychology, 17*(2), 89–100.

Bruner, J. S. (1979). *On knowing: Essays for the left hand*. Cambridge, MA: Harvard University Press.

Bruner, J. S. (1979). Preschool observations. *Concern: Journal of National Children's Bureau, 33*, 16–21.

Bruner, J. S. (1980). Jerome S. Bruner. In G. Lindzey (Ed.), *History of psychology in autobiography*, Vol. 7 (pp. 75–151). San Francisco: W. H. Freeman.

Bruner, J. S. (1980). *Under five in Britain*. London: Grant McIntyre.

Bruner, J. S. (1983). *Child's talk: Learning to use language*. New York: W. W. Norton.

Bruner, J. S. (1983). *In search of mind: Essays in autobiography*. New York: Harper and Row Publishing.

Bruner, J. S. (1985). Models of the learner. *Educational Researcher, 14*(6), 5–8.

Bruner, J. S. (1985). On teaching thinking: An afterthought. In S. F. Chipman, J. W. Segal, & R. Glaser (Eds.), *Thinking and learning skills (Vol. 2): Research and open questions* (pp. 597–608). Hillsdale, NJ: Lawrence Erlbaum Associates.

Bruner, J. S. (1986). *Actual minds, possible worlds*. Cambridge, MA: Harvard University Press.

Bruner, J. S. (1990). *Acts of meaning*. Cambridge, MA: Harvard University Press.

Bruner, J. S. (1991). The meaning of educational reform. *National Association of Montessori Teachers Journal (Special edition: Schools of thought: Pathways to educational reform), 16*(2), 29–40.

Bruner, J. S. (1992). Science education and teachers: A Karplus lecture. *Journal of Science Education and Technology, 1*(1), 5–12.

Bruner, J. S. (1993). Explaining and interpreting: Two ways of using mind. In G. Harman (Ed.), *Conceptions of the human mind: Essays in honor of George A. Miller* (pp. 123–137). Hillsdale, NJ: Lawrence Erlbaum Associates.

Olson, D. R., & Bruner, J. S. (1996). Folk psychology and folk pedagogy. In D. R. Olson & N. Torrance (Eds.), *The handbook of education and human development* (pp. 9–27). Cambridge, MA: Blackwell.

Bruner, J. S. (1996). *The culture of education*. Cambridge, MA: Harvard University Press.

Bruner, J. S. (1996). What we have learned about early learning. *European Early Childhood Education Research Journal, 4*(1), 5–16.

Bruner, J. S. (1997). Keeping the conversation going: An interview with Jerome Bruner, with Bradd Shore. *Ethos, 25*(1), 7–62.

Bruner, J. S. (1997). What are we learning about learning in schools? In B. S. Kogan (Ed.), *Common schools, uncommon futures: A working consensus for school renewal.* New York: Teachers College Press.

Bruner, J. S. (1999, April). *Early childhood pedagogy.* Keynote address presented at the Conference on Early Pedagogy in Global Perspective, National Academy of Science.

Bruner, J. S. (1999). Postscript: Some reflections on educational research. In E. C. Lagemann & L. S. Shulman (Eds.), *Issues in educational research: Problems and possibilities* (pp. 399–409). San Francisco: Jossey-Bass.

Bruner, J. S. (2000). Foreword. In J. S. DeLoache and A. Gottlieb (Eds.). *A world of babies: Imagined childcare guides for seven societies.* Cambridge: Cambridge University Press.

Bruner, J. S. (2000, March 9). Tot thought: A review of The scientist in the crib and The myth of the first three years. *The New York Review of Books, 47*(4), 27–30.

Amsterdam, A. G., & Bruner, J. S. (2000). *Minding the law.* Cambridge, MA: Harvard University Press.

Bruner, J. S. (2001). In response. In D. Bakhurst and S. Shanker (Eds.), *Jerome Bruner: Language, culture, self* (pp. 199–215). London: Sage Publications.

Bruner, J. S. (n.d.) *Bruner Papers.* Housed in the Harvard University Archives, Cambridge, MA.

Bruner, J. S. (in press). [Making stories: Law, literature, life]. New York: Farrar Strauss Giroux.

Sources by Others

America's Future. (1996). *What matters most: Teaching for America's future.* New York: Author.

Barry, N., & Orlofsky, D. (1994). The effect of sequential instruction upon elementary education majors' ability to match pitch and perform prescribed song-leading tasks. *PMEA Bulletin of Research in Music Education, 19*, 23–33.

Berliner, D. C. (2000). A personal response to those who bash teacher education. *Journal of Teacher Education, 51*(5), 358–371.

Brown, A. L. (1988). Motivation to learn and understand: On taking charge of one's own learning. *Cognition and Instruction, 5*(4), 311–321.

Brown, A. L. (1994). The advancement of learning. *Educational Researcher, 23*(8), 4–12.

Brown, A. L., & Campione, J. C. (1990). Communities of learning and thinking, or a context by any other name. In D. Kuhn (Ed.), *Developmental perspectives on teaching and learning thinking skills* (pp. 108–126). Basel: Karger.

Brown, C. A. (1995, April). *Beyond the spiral curriculum: Jerome Bruner's cognitive journey and its implications for music education.* Paper presented at the Indiana Symposium in Interdisciplinary Perspectives on Music Education, Bloomington, IN.

Carnegie Forum. (1986). *A nation prepared: Teachers for the 21st century.* New York: Author.

Darling-Hammond, L. (1999). Educating teachers: The academy's greatest failure or its most important future? *Academe, 85*(1), 26–33.

DeNicola, D. N. (1986). The development of an instructional language assessment instrument based upon the historical perspectives of Quintilian, Erasmus, and Herbart and its use in analyzing the language behaviors of preservice elementary and music education majors. (Doctoral dissertation, Florida State University, 1986). *Dissertation Abstracts International, 47*, 08A.

DeNicola, D. N. (1990). Historical perspectives on instructional language as applied to an assessment of preservice teachers. *Journal of Research in Music Education, 38*(1), 49–60.

DeNicola, D. N. (1990). *The development and evaluation of a twelve-step sequential method to teach class piano sightreading.* Paper presented to the Music Educators National Conference Southern Division Convention, Winston-Salem, NC.

DeNicola, D. N. (1991). In memoriam. *Proteus: A Journal of Ideas, 8*(1), 16–17.

Durant, W. (1953). *The story of philosophy.* New York: Simon and Schuster.

Ehrenberg, L. (1983). How to ensure better transfer of learning. *Training and Development Journal, 37.*

Farkas, S., & Johnson, J. (1997). *Different drummers: How teachers of teachers view public education.* New York: The Public Agenda.

Feldman, S. (1999). Only connect: Professors and teachers with a common mission. *Academe, 85*(1), 22–25.

Fullan, M., Galluzzo, G., Morris, P., & Watson, N. (1998). *The rise and stall of teacher education reform.* Washington, DC: AACTE Publications.

Gagné, R. M. (1965). *The conditions of learning.* New York: Holt, Rinehart and Winston.

Gardner, H. (1985). *Frames of mind.* New York: Basic Books.

Goleman, D. (1995). *Emotional intelligence.* New York: Bantam Books.

Goodlad, J. I. (1999). Whither schools of education? *Journal of Teacher Education, 50*(5), 325ff.

Gopnik, A. (1990). Knowing, doing and talking: The Oxford years. *Human Development, 33,* 338.

Hatano, G., & Inagaki, K. (1987). A theory of motivation for comprehension and its application to mathematics instruction. In T. A. Romberg & D. N. Steward (Eds.), *The monitoring of school mathematics: Background papers, Vol. 2. Implications from psychology, outcomes of instruction* (Program Rep. No. 87-2, pp. 27–66). Madison: Wisconsin Center for Educational Research.

The Holmes Group. (1986). *Tomorrow's teachers: A report of the Holmes Group.* East Lansing, MI: Author.

The Holmes Group. (1990). *Tomorrow's schools: Principles for the design of PDS.* East Lansing, MI: Author.

The Holmes Group. (1995). *Tomorrow's schools of education: A report of the Holmes Group.* East Lansing, MI: Author.

Koprowicz, C. (1996). Teaching our teachers. *State Legislatures, 22*(10), 20–24.

Labaree, D. F. (1999). Too easy a target: The trouble with ed schools and the implications for the university. *Academe, 85*(1), 34–39.

Lewis, L., Farris, E., Parsad, B., Carey, N., Smerdon, B., Bartfai, N., Westat, Pelavin Research Center, & American Institutes for Research. (1999, January). *Teacher quality: A report on the preparation and qualifications of public school teachers.* Retrieved May 5, 2000 from the World Wide Web: www.nces.ed.gov/pub99/1999080.html.

Madsen, C. K., & Kuhn, T. L. (1994). *Contemporary music education.* Raleigh, NC: Contemporary Publishing Company.

Madsen, C. H., & Madsen, C. K. (1981). *Teaching/discipline: A positive approach for educational development* (3rd ed.). Raleigh, NC: Contemporary Publishing.

Maher, F., & Tetreault, M. K. (1999). Knowledge versus pedagogy: The marginalization of teacher education. *Academe, 85*(1), 40–43.

Mertz, M. (1999). Using portfolios: Assessment, review, evaluation. *ATE Newsletter, 32*(3), 4–5.

Orlofsky, D. (1996). Cavemen used music like phones. *National Forum, 76*(1), 7–8.

Orlofsky, D. (1997). Going behind the notes. *Clavier, 36*(9), 9–11, 24.

Orlofsky, D., & Lyda, R. (2001). *Working together: A look at collaborative learning in two different settings.* Manuscript submitted for presentation consideration.

Papert, S. (1999, March 29). Jean Piaget. *Time, 153,* 105–107.

Perrone, V. (1991). *A letter to teachers.* San Francisco: Jossey-Bass.

Posner, G. J., & Rudnitsky, A. N. (1997). *Course design: A guide to curriculum development for teachers* (5th ed.). New York: Longman.

Rhodes, L. K., & Bellamy, G. T. (1999). Choices and consequences in the renewal of teacher education. *Journal of Teacher Education, 50,* 17.

Rigden, D. W. (1996). *What teachers have to say about teacher education*. Washington, DC: Council for Basic Education; and National Commission on Teaching.

Riley, R. W. (1999, February). *New challenges, a new resolve: Moving American education into the 21st century*. Sixth annual State of American Education speech, Long Beach, CA.

Shore, B. (1997). Keeping the conversation going: An interview with Jerome Bruner. *Ethos, 25*(1), 7–62.

Valli, L., & Rennert-Arriev, P. L. (2000). Identifying consensus in teacher education reform documents: A proposed framework and action implications. *Journal of Teacher Education, 51*(1), 5–17.

Welton, B. (1999). The message and the medium: The roots/routes of Jerome Bruner's Postmodernism. *Theory and Research in Social Education, 27*(2), 169–178.

Whitehead, A. N. (1932). *The aims of education and other essays*. London: Williams and Northgate.

Wise, A. E. (2000). Performance-based accreditation: Reform in action. *The Newsletter of the National Council for Accreditation of Teacher Education, 9*(2), 1–2.

Index